4 Steps Through the Narrow Gate

Margaret St. Peter

Published by Narrow Path Books

PO Box 69563 Tucson, Az 85737

narrowpathbooks@icloud.com

ISBN: 978-1-07-724838-0

Author photo: Brian Halbach
Cover photo: Natalie Irwin
Editor: Phyllis White
Advisor: Lew White
Encouragers: Sharon Kaste, Karel Thomas, Betti Fernandez, Natalie Irwin

Print and eBook editions available at Amazon.com

Visit Margaret St. Peter author page
Facebook: www.facebook.com/margaret.st.peter.5686

4 Steps Through the Narrow Gate

This is the Way… Walk in It

Margaret St. Peter

To Yahusha
For Yahusha's Joy

•   •   •

CONTENTS

LETTER PACKAGE 4: TESTIMONY OF YAHUSHA

FOREWORD

This work is truly blessed by Yahusha. Finally, under one cover is the Scriptural source for knowing not only the True Name of our Creator, but the importance of knowing that Name and getting it right. So many people have said "He knows what I mean." Try saying that to your significant other.

I've only known Margaret for a little more than a year and already she is teaching me things I've wondered about for 30 years. The Insights that Yahusha has given her are amazing and the conclusions she brings in these writings, are astounding. Prepare yourself to have your eyes and heart opened to the calling of our Awesome Father Yahusha!

Reading Through the Narrow Gate Letters contained in this book, one can focus on how they should live to please Yahusha. It will also open your eyes to many truths that you may miss simply by reading through the Scriptures. A Shepherd once wrote in Tehillim (Psalms) 119 vs 105 "Your Word is a lamp to my feet and a Light to my path." Yashayahu (Isaiah) wrote in chapter 30 vs 21 "and your ears hear a word behind you, saying, 'This is the Way, walk in it,' whenever you turn to the right, or whenever you turn to the left."

Staying on the narrow path means that you will not be doing what everyone else is doing. Yirmeyahu (Jeremiah) 10 vs 2: Thus, said Yahuah, "do not learn the way of the gentiles, and do not be awed by the signs of the shamayim, for the gentiles are awed by them." We are the bride of Yahusha and we will walk in His ways.

Margaret's book, Through the Narrow Gate, is a must read for everyone living in these trying times. It will be a comfort as well as a guide and open your eyes to many things you may have missed.

Phyllis White

X

INTRODUCTION

Around the turn of the century (1999 to 2000) I really began to wonder about the foundations of faith. What were they really and where are they in the scripture? What I discovered was very different than what was being taught everywhere, in all the different congregations. I found that each religious organization had their own slant on the foundations of faith to match their man-created doctrines and rules. I earned my master's degree studying the foundation of faith and I came away from that journey more convinced than ever what I learned was missing something. That something turned out to be complete truth! There are many deviations from truth being taught.

My quest to understand the foundation of faith was to know how to gain enteral life. At that time, I was concerned about the loud voices condemning everyone to hell if their way was not followed. Fear and getting older drove me forward to search for the truth.

In 2018 my search for truth was answered. The scripture that tells us to knock and the door will be open proved real in my life. My personality is to readily share what I learn with others. Really, I have exhausted my friends on this because like YirmeYahu 20:9 I cannot keep this truth shut up in my bones. I decided I just had to write what I had learned and eventually realized the writing needed to be turned into a book! This is the book from the letters I wrote as the Spirit of Yahusha taught me.

The foundations of faith turned out to be a path through the narrow gate and what could be a difficult path in the day in which we live because it is contrary to the norm. (Matthew 7:14) I have found because I have set my heart on this path it is not as difficult as one might imagine. It all depends on your dedication and choices. Which is true of any goal you set your heart on. Like Paul (Philippians 3:14) let us set our hearts on the goal and press forward. Choose to follow his advice.

The foundations of faith I sought have now become the narrow gate and way. There is so much joy in knowing our Creator and Savior. I think this will be true for you also. Some of these letters seem simple but it is the whole of the letters that will show you the narrow gate to go through and the how of walking the focused path. There is only one teacher, the Spirit of Yahusha. As Paul encouraged Timothy, I too encourage you that the goal of this book is love from a pure heart and a good conscience with sincere faith to bring truth to you. (1 Timothy 1:5)

For Yahusha's Joy,
Margaret a Natsari

A MESSAGE FROM MY MENTOR

When the Truth is heard and tested, we become responsible to safe-guard it, be trained by it, and to live in it, because the Day of Yahuah is coming closer with each passing moment.

The Truth is a Person and calling on His Name seals us for the day of our redemption.

If received, the Truth is able to repair the breach, and restore us to favor. Shouting what was whispered in the inner rooms from the rooftops will expose the false reasoning of the principalities impris-oning the minds of billions for many centuries. This will draw the rage of the dragon.

The things men build, and think are precious are an abomination to Yahuah. (see Luke 16:15)

They have made their own way, and built their strong towers, but Yahuah says, *"Unless Yahuah builds the house, its builders labor in vain."*

On 4-15-2019 as the building dedicated to "our lady of Paris" smoldered, hundreds of millions of dollars were donated to rebuild it. What needs to be repaired is the breach between mankind and Yahuah, by receiving and obeying the Truth, Yahuah's Word. A resto-ration of Yahuah's greatest creation is now beginning. Humanity is witnessing the fulfillment of predictions given to us by Yahusha at Mt. 24, and we are here to warn all who will listen to our message: "Repent! The Day of Yahuah draws near."

We are all of the repairers of the breach, assisting Yahusha as He prepares for His bride. Though we are weak and pressed on every side, we know the battle is Yahuah's, and no weapon formed can prevail against us. (see YashaYahu / Isaiah 54:17)

He uses each of us to smooth some wrinkles, so His inheritance becomes a clean, bright, spotless bride, blessed by His adornments, cleansed by His blood.

As the dragon attacks and rages on, Yahusha is shielding us from the fiery arrows. Revelation 12:17 says the dragon wages war on us because we are obedient to the Commandments, and testify of our trust in Yahusha.

As it is written, *"For your sake we are being killed all day long; we are regarded as sheep to be slaughtered."* (Romans 8:36, Psalm 44:22)

This is how we know we know Him: if we guard His Commandments. (see 1 Yahukanon / 1 John 2:4)

As you read, listen with Yahusha's Mind and purpose, not your own, or what men taught you to think. When you do, He will transform you into a useful vessel for Him to use.

> *I have been impaled with Mashiak, and I no longer live,*
> *but Mashiak lives in me. And that which I now live in the*
> *flesh I live by belief in the Son of Yahuah, who loved me*
> *and gave Himself for me.*
>
> GALATIANS 2:20 BYNV

Lew White
author of *Fossilized Customs*
www.fossilizedcustoms.net

• • •

LETTER PACKAGE 1:
THE NAME

. . .

LETTER 1:
INTRODUCTION TO THE NAME

I am Yahuah, that is My Name
And My esteem I do not give to another,
Nor My praise to idols.

YASHAYAHU 42:8 BYNV

Greetings From: A Natsari, Follower of Yahusha
To You: Discovering the Way of the Natsarim

Teaching letters are short insightful sharing of the Scriptures to help all of us grow in the likeness of Yahusha. These letters come from my time spent with the Scriptures of Truth and additional studies.

My journey to understanding the narrow gate and path has been well over 20 years. The scripture of truth tells us that we must find the narrow gate if we are to see Yahuah. As understanding was revealed to me, I have been deeply affected. This life changing understanding drew me into an urgent desire to share these understandings with others, like you. Just as Paul wrote letters to those he loved, I have been captive in my home for about a year writing these letters to you because of the love of Yahusha.

These truths will challenge the understandings you have grown up with. There are many changes, slight deviations from the original Hebrew scripture that have affected what we have all learned to be truth. In these letters, you will be amazed at the correct translation of Scripture and how that changes everything. Come along with me, from letter to letter, learning as the followers of Yahusha did so long ago. You too, will be filled with a deep desire and urgency to share all you learn. As this is the beginning, we will begin with the very basic most important thing.

We have all read in the scripture that *"Those who know me know my voice."* We have also read *"This is my name call me by my name,"* and *"Many will come and say Lord, Lord I knew you,"* Matithyahu (Matthew) 7:21–23) and he will answer them get away from me I do not know you and *"because the gate is narrow, and the way is hard pressed which leads to life, and there are few who find* it." Matithyahua (Matthew) 7:14

These particular snippets Scriptures have always been of concern to me to know the details of how these things could happen. I have been unable to find answers, satisfying answers in our current translations that we call the Bible and that is because the translations are not quite clear and do not exactly line up with the original words and teachings of Yahusha.

In this first letter, I am going to share with you the correct names for the one you call God and the one you call Jesus. In my next letter I will give you more detailed understanding of the error that we have all taken as truth. (You may have a slight different spellings and pronunciations of The Name. Let's not judge by what I have received as right. You might prefer a different variation of the Name but still one of the accepted Hebrew translations.)

The creator of the universe, the almighty one's correct name is Yahuah (ya hoo ah).

YashaYahu (Isaiah) 42:8: *"I am Yahuah, that is My Name, and My esteem I do not give to another, nor my praise to idols." YashaYahu (Isaiah) 42:8 BYNV*

The Deliverer sent by Yahuah to be the living sacrifice for our redemption name is

Yahusha (Ya hoo sha)

Meaning: Yahuah is Deliverer. I am your Deliverer.

In the next letter we will discover Mosheh's (Moses) experience with Alahim and how Mosheh learned The NAME by which all were to address the Creator.

For Yahusha's Joy,
A Natsari

LETTER 2:
MOSHEH AND THE NAME

*In the previous letter the Hebrew Names of our
Creator and our Savior were revealed. In this
letter we will discover when we were first told to
use The Name and how important it is that we do.*

Greetings From: A Natsari, Follower of Yahusha
To You: Discovering the Way of the Natsarim

The name of our Creator and our Deliverer are not the names you
see in your Bible (Scripture of Truth) every day.

Let's look at this and see what we find. We will begin with the
Torah or the first 5 books of the Scripture of Truth which were written by Moses (Mosheh). The purpose of the Torah is to teach us love
for Yahuah and love for our neighbor. The Torah is about relationship. Yahuah is about relationship.

Our first stop in the Torah is Exodus (Shemoth)20. The Alahim
spoke to Mosheh laying out the 10 rules/covenants of the marriage
contract between the Hebrew people and Yahuah. This is the time
when Mosheh when up Mt. Sinai and received the stone tablet with
the marriage covenant or what you may call the 10 commandments.

(Recently I was reading the account of that event and saw for the
first time that Mosheh ascended that mountain 3 times, staying for
40 days and nights each time. 1st He went up for 40 days and nights

and he brought the tablets down. He broke them because his frustration with their disobedience. 2nd Then he went up and entreated Alahim for the people. He stayed another 40 days and nights. 3rd He had to make new tablets and take them up. He again stayed 40 days and night. And his face shone on his return. Mosheh then kept his face vailed except when before Alahim in the Tent of Meetings)

The very first commands talks about the Name and behaviors they were to keep regarding Yahuah their Alahim.

This is a long passage, but it is important to understand it, so the passage follows:

And Alahim spoke all these Words, saying,

Shemoth (Exodus) 20 1- 7

> *1 I am Yahuah your Alahim, who brought you out of the land of Egypt (Mitsrayim), out of the house of slavery.*
>
> *2 You have no other mighty ones against My face.*
>
> *3 You do not make for yourself a carved image, or any likeness of that which is in the heavens (shamayim) above, or which is in the earth (arets) beneath, or which is in the seas (mayim under the arets).*
>
> *4 You do not bow down to them nor serve them.*
>
> *5 For I, Yahuah your Alahim am a jealous Al, visiting the crookedness of the fathers on the children to the 3rd and 4th generations of those who hate Me,*
>
> *6 but showing kindness to thousands, to those who love Me and guard my commands.*
>
> *7 You do not cast the name of Yahuah you Alahim to ruin (vain).*
>
> SHEMOTH (EXODUS) 20:1–7 BYNV

Hold this in your memory because we will come back to it often in the letters.

Now we are going to pick up another piece of understanding to hold onto as we progress. We are going back in the Torah when this whole adventure between Mosheh and Yahuah began. You may remember the story of the burning bush (Shemoth 3) and Mosheh caught his sight and then he turned to see what this burning but not consumed bush was all about. When he did a voice from the bush spoke to him.

Shemoth (Exodus) 3:2-4:

> 2 And the Messenger of Yahuah appeared to him in a flame of fire from the midst of a bush.
>
> And he looked and saw the bush burning with fire, but the bush was not consumed.
>
> 3 And Mosheh said, "Let me turn aside now, and see this great sight, why the bush does not burn."
>
> 4 And Yahuah saw that he turned aside to see, and Alahim called to him from the midst of the bush and said, "Mosheh! Mosheh!" And he said, "Here I am."
>
> SHEMOTH (EXODUS) 3:2-4 BYNV

Shemoth (Exodus) 3:6:

> 6 And he said, "I am the Alahim of your father, the Alahim of Abraham, the Alahim of Yitshaq (Isaac), and the Alahim of YaAqob (Jacob). [about this moment Mosheh realizes who is speaking to him and he gets a holy fear come over him, and rightfully so] And Mosheh hid his face, for he was afraid to look at Alahim.
>
> SHEMOTH (EXODUS) 3:6 BYNV

The chapter continues with the conversation between Yahuah and Mosheh. The short of it is that Mosheh learns he has been selected to lead the Hebrew people out of captivity from the Egyptians (Mitsrites). As Yahuah unfolds, what I call Mosheh's marching orders, Mosheh becomes concerned about The Name he will use to describe the mighty one who is demanding Farah release the Hebrew slaves from Mitsrayim. Mosheh has a valid reason for this need. The Mitsrites who worshipped many gods had names for their gods and Mosheh needed to have a name. Mosheh's first approach with Yahuah is found in verse 13,

Shemoth (Exodus)3:13–15

> *13 And Mosheh said to Alahim, "See, when I come to the children of Yisharal (Israel) and say to them, 'The Alahim of your fathers has sent me to you,' and they say to me, 'What is His Name?' what shall I say to them?"*
>
> *14 And Alahim said to Mosheh,*
>
> **Ahayah Asher Ahayah,**
> **(I will be Who I will be)**
>
> *And He said, "Thus you shall say to the children of Yisharal, AHAYAH has sent me to you.*
>
> *15 "And Alahim said further to Mosheh, "Thus you are to say to the children of Yisharal, Yahuah of your fathers, the Alahim of Abraham, the Alahim of Yitshaq, and the Alahim of YaAqob has sent me to you. This is My Name forever, and this is MY remembrance to all generations."*
>
> SHEMOTH (EXODUS)3:13 -15 BYNV

Are you a part of "all generations"? Yes, you are, therefore the correct name for you to use when referring to the creator of the universe is **Yahuah (Ya Hoo ah).** Now you know The Name!

There is much more to discover. In our next letter you will find out how The Name was silenced and hidden.

For Yahusha's Joy,
A Natsari

LETTER 3:
THE NAME IS SILENCED

In the previous letter we learned when The Name was given. We also learned that Yahuah would be His name forever and He would not share his praise with another. His name is a remembrance to all generations.

Greetings From: A Natsari, Follower of Yahusha
To You: Discovering the Way of the Natsarim

In this letter we will uncover the mystery surrounding the disappearance of Yahuah's name. Let's look at a couple of scriptures that were spoken by the prophets that told of things to come.

YashaYahu (Isaiah) 52.6

> "*Therefore, My people shall know My Name, in that yom (day), for I am the One who is speaking. See, it is I, Yahuah*"
>
> YASHAYAHU (ISAIAH) 52.6 BYNV

YashaYahu (Isaiah) 42:8

> *I am Yahuah, that is My Name, and My esteem I do not give to another, nor My praise to idols.*"
>
> YASHAYAHU (ISAIAH) 42:8 BYNV

YashaYahu (Isaiah) 43:11

I, I am Yahuah, and besides Me there is no deliverer.

YASHAYAHU (ISAIAH) 43:11 BYNV

The one thing that was really made clear to the House of Israel was the correct Name of Alahim. No matter what was to happen they knew His Name and they knew they should not share His esteem with another.

In their captivity they lost sight of this most important thing. Christianity today has lost sight of this most important thing, too. The Name is Hebrew, there is no English equal for it. All languages are to use The Name in Hebrew.

We cannot be ok with using the word 'God' for Yahuah as you will come to understand.

One of the first commands of Yahuah was to not eat flesh with the life (blood) in it. Barashith (Genesis) 9:4 This command was given to Noak (Noah) after the flood. The next important command was to use His Name given to Mosheh (Moses) Shemoth (Exodus) 3:15.

YirmeYahu (Jeremiah) the prophet had a message in chapter 19/20 for Pashhur son of Amar, the priest who was also chief governor in the House of Yahuah. Pashhur had him put in stocks because he did not like the message. The next day Pashhur brought YirmeYahu (Jeremiah) to him and YirmeYahu (Jeremiah) basically told him the people of Yahudah were going to be given over to the sovereign of Babel and it was not going to be a pretty sight because they had forsaken Yahuah and had burned incense to other mighty ones whom their ancestors had not known. This is the reason why they were taken into captivity.

The Yahudim (Jewish) people had forgotten their first love. They had forgotten who they were betrothed to and had taken up with the pagan gods. This was completely against what they had been commanded in YashaYahu (Isaiah) 42:8. YirmeYahu (Jeremiah) was more than distraught.

YirmeYahu (Jeremiah) 20:7–9

> 7 Oh Yahuah, You enticed me, and I was enticed. You are stronger than I and have prevailed. I have been ridiculed all yom (day) long, everyone mocks me.
>
> 8 For when I speak, I cry out, proclaiming violence and ruin. Because the Word of Yahuah was made to me a reproach and a derision (mocking) daily.
>
> 9 Whenever I said, "Let me not mention Him, nor speak in His Name again," it was in my heart like a burning fire shut up in my bones. And I became wearily of holding it back and was helpless.
>
> YIRMEYAHU (JEREMIAH) 20:7–9 BYNV

What was happening to YirmeYahu (Jeremiah) happens to all of us, once we know The Name. We cannot keep the understanding to ourselves. We must share The Name. It is like fire shut up in our bones.

The House of Yahudah had begun to exchange the true Name of Yahuah for the Kananite storm deity named Baal. In Hebrew Baal means Lord. They were mixing worship. They were giving praise, that belonged to Yahuah to the pagan god, Baal (Lord).

Did you catch that. The meaning of the Kananite deity, Baal was *Lord* in Hebrew.

The word Lord has carried through the generations because of the KJV version. "Lord" has become a common word to identify the Almighty One.

Every time we proclaim the word "Lord" we are proclaiming the name of the deity of the Kananite people; Baal.

Just ponder that for a bit. Let that roll over your heart. Who are you praising and proclaiming? Are you breaking the 3rd Commandment? I know it shocked me when I learned what I was doing. I have since corrected myself to proclaim Yahuah. And I will share with you, it takes a couple of weeks to get your mind and mouth using the correct name because it has been taught to us from a very young age. Do not worry your friends and family will accept that you have changed how you address the Creator. They may not make the same choice however every time they hear you, you are planting the seed in them to do the same.

I am offended for Yahuah when I hear people refer to The Creator as "Lord", my heart is pierced when He is called "God."

The Yahudim had begun this behavior of mixing worship and they did not change their behavior when YirmeYahu told them what was going to happen. Have you noticed, the 10 commandments are to help us with our behavior? They are not hard to do, we have just been taught that they are hard to keep. They show us how to love Yahuah and how to behave toward each other.

YirmeYahu (Jeremiah) 23:25–27

> *25 I have heard what the prophets have said who prophesy falsehood in My Name, saying, 'I have dreamed, I have dreamed!'*
>
> *26 the prophets of falsehood and prophets of the deceit of their own heart,*
>
> *27 who try to make My people forget My Name by their dreams which everyone relates to his neighbor, as their fathers forgot My Name for Baal.*
>
> YIRMEYAHU (JEREMIAH) 23:25–27 BYNV

Yahuah could no longer take their worship of other deities. He removed His Name from their lips and ripped it out of their hearts by the root. This would come to pass when they were handed over to the sovereign of Babel.

And it happened, they were taken into bondage by the sovereign of Babel. This is how it happened:

The people of Babel were a pagan people. They had their deities they worshiped but they did not share the name of their deities with everyone. You had to be in the upper ranks to be allowed to know and use the name of the deity. The people of Babel believed if others knew the name of their deity then they would have power over them. They used code words to refer to their deities.

Yahuah was not afraid for his people to use his name. NO ONE would ever have power over Him or His people, if his people remained true to Him and His Name. The problem was not with Yahuah, the problem was with the Yahudim. Their behavior brought to pass what Yahuah had proclaimed in heaven.

The pagans began to bully the House of Israel about using The Name and basically made fun of The Name. The Pharisees and the scribes, the teaching authority of their day, decided that no one would use the name Yahuah. They went so far as to impose death by stoning on anyone who did use The Name.

How did they replace The Name? The use Adonai (my sovereign) and later they used YESHU. Yeshu is an acronym. The letters in this acronym mean: **may his name be blotted out.**

This term, Yeshu, is used in the Yahudim's ancient writings from their Rabbi called the Talmud. They treasure the traditions the Talmud. Yahuah does not treasure man's traditions — He hates them.

Now the Pharisees had put into place the silencing of The Name and the punishment for using The Name. Over the time in captivity the people adhered to the governing of the Pharisees and Yahuah's name was silenced as He had proclaimed in Heaven.

There were some in the Yahudim who were not satisfied with just the silencing and punishment. They wanted to be sure for generations to come, that no one would uncover The Name. In our next Letter we will find out:

- who they were
- how they did it
- how what they did affects us even today

We will also learn exactly when Yahuah brought His name back to the lips of the Natarsim.

For Yahusha's Joy,
A Natsari

LETTER 4:
INFLUENCE OF MASORETES

In our last Letter we learned that Yahuah removed
His Name from the hearts of Israel because they
had "cast the Name of Yahuah you Alahim to ruin."

Greetings From: A Natsari, Follower of Yahusha
To You: Discovering the Way of the Natsarim

In this letter we will see what was done by man to attempt to make this change permanent.

When the Babylonian captivity was over and a portion of Israel (Yahudim) returned to Yerushalayim (Jerusalem), I wonder why the governing power, the Pharisees, did not return the proper Name to its Glory. History does not record an effort to do so therefore The Name remained hidden. I can only believe this happened because it was not Yahuah's desire that it should be restored. Yahuah had a greater plan and purpose to come.

One of the actions of the Pharisees was to declare that if anyone did use the Name, such behavior would be punishable by death. What is recorded is the possibly deliberate and successful attempt by a sect of Yahudim to permanently silence the Name and totally change how Hebrew is written and spoken.

We know that during the House of Yahudah's 70-year captivity, The Name became hidden for 2 reasons:

1. The influence of Pagan custom of hiding the name of their deities. The House of Yahudah's inclining toward mixed worship, evidence of which we still see today.

2. Yahuah named His people Yahudim, after himself. Daniel 9:19. So even though they tried to hide his name, they were unique because their people group carried His Name within their people group name. The pagans used the Name of Yahuah in jest, and that was outrageous to the Yahudim causing the Pharisees to silence The Name and impose the death penalty.

When did Yahuah place His name on His people? The answer is clearly shown in Scripture although we may not have realized what this popular blessing was really doing.

Bamidbar (Numbers) 6:22–27

> *22 And Yahuah spoke to Mosheh, saying:*
>
> *23 Speak to Aharon and his sons, saying, "This is how you bless the children of Yisharal. Say to them:*
>
> *24 Yahuah bless you and guard you;*
>
> *25 Yahuah make His face shine upon you, and show favor to you;*
>
> *26 Yahuah lift up His face upon you and give you shalom."*
>
> *27 Thus, they shall put My Name on their children of Yisharal, and I Myself shall bless them.*
>
> BAMIDBAR (NUMBERS) 6:22–27 BYNV

The pagans attack on Yahuah's Name was so intense for the Yahudim that they stopped using His Name and even made using it punishable by death. They used instead Adonai meaning my sovereign.

There was a Karaite sext of traditionalists that became zealous to protect The Name or maybe to hide the name. The Masoretes, 6 -11 BCE, were scribes and they copied the Scripture of Truth for the Yahudim. The Karate sext was an ultra-traditionalist group who was concerned with the integrity of the Scripture of Truth. They took it upon themselves to invent vowel-points in order for people to pronounce Hebrew words correctly. Many argue today that Hebrew does not have vowels but that is not the truth. Flavius Josephus (Yusef ben MatithYahu) shows us in his historic writings that the Name of our Creator was written in qodesh letters consisting of four vowels.

These vowels are: Yod-Hay-Uau-Hay

Before we leave this Letter I want to bring your attention to the importance of Yahuah's position regarding His Name. We should take note of what Yahuah was saying to all mankind not only his chosen people.

Tehillim (Psalms) 79:6

> *6 Pour out your wrath on the nations who have not known you, and on reigns that have not called on Your Name.*
>
> TEHILLIM (PSALMS) 79:6 BYNV

YashaYahu (Isaiah) 42:8

> *42 I am Yahuah, that is My Name, and My esteem I do not give to another, nor my praise to idols.*
>
> YASHAYAHU (ISAIAH) 42:8 BYNV

YashaYahu (Isaiah) 43:11

> *11 I, I am Yahuah, and besides Me there is no Deliverer.*
>
> YASHAYAHU (ISAIAH) 43:11BYNV

Around the world we find many different names for Yahuah. These are the names of men. The Scripture of Truth clearly shows The Name, Yahuah. It is a Hebrew name, there is not an equal name in any other language. All men are to use The Name; Yahuah when referring to the Almighty Alahim.

In the next letter, we will discover when Yahuah brought His Name back and the reaction the Yahudim had to this great event.

For Yahusha's Joy,
A Natsari

Note:

I researched the Masoretes on line and found information on www.aleppocodex.org which will give you a broader understanding of their role.

The goal of the Masoretes was to guard and preserve the text of the Bible, which had been handed down from generation to genera-tion. To achieve this goal, the Masoretes worked in several parallel directions, and in the end, they were highly successful. The Masoretes worked to determine the text of the Scripture. They stated the proper way of writing and reading the Scripture, and in passages where they found differences between texts and ways of reading, they issued a decision and ruled as to which opinion was correct. These decisions related not only to verses and words, but to every single letter.

One of the important projects of the Masoretes was the invention of vowel marks for the Hebrew language. Hebrew writing is mainly consonantal. Auxiliary letters, alef, vav, and yod are occasionally used to indicate the vowel sound, but they only can be used for some of the vowels, and those vowels cannot be indicated unambiguously by the auxiliary letters.

2 4

LETTER 5:
YAHUAH PROCLAIMED!

*In our last Letter we learned how Yahuah's name
was hidden in the Scripture by the Pharisees and
even more effectively by the Masoretes.*

Greetings From: A Natsari, Follower of Yahusha
To You: Discovering the Way of the Natsarim

In this letter we will see when Yahuah re-announced His Name and
who announced it.

Let's look at Luke 4 beginning at verse 16. In this Scripture Yahusha is reading from YashaYahu (Isaiah) and proclaims he is the one
that has been sent.

Luke 4:16

> *16 And he came to Natsarith, where He had been brought
> up. And according to His practice, He went into the
> congregation on the yom Shabath, and stood up to read.
> The scroll of the prophet YashaYahu (Isaiah) was handed
> to Him. And having unrolled the scroll, he found the place
> where it was written:*

> *The Ruach (spirit) of Yahuah is upon Me, because He
> has appointed Me, (Aleph/Tav meaning strength of the*

covenant or he has appointed me by the "hand of the
Almighty") to bring the besorah (message) to the broken-
hearted, to proclaim release to the captives and recovery
of sight to the blind, to send away crushed ones with a
release, to proclaim the acceptable year of the Yahuah...
Today this Scripture has been concluded in your hearing.

LUKE 4:16 BYNV

In this statement Yahusha is proclaiming Yahuah, which in the scroll he was reading The Name had been replaced and silenced. By most accounts, this was the moment Yahuah re-introduced His name to the common Yahudim. Yahusha said He was the one Yahuah had sent to fulfill this Scripture. This did not sit well with the Pharisees and was the beginning of the Pharisees desire to be rid of Yahusha.

Luke 9:1

1 And having called His 12 pupils together, He gave
them power and authority over all demons, and to heal
diseases. And he sent them to proclaim the reign of
Yahuah and to heal the sick.

LUKE 9:1 BYNV

Again, Yahusha is proclaiming Yahuah's rightful name and He is instructing his pupils, who you know as the apostles, to proclaim the "reign of Yahuah." They were bold to bring back The Name of Yahuah. When you read the chapters where Yahusha is teaching the multitude of people he was speaking to them about the reign of Yahuah, (Luke 9:11)

It is clear that one of the main works Yahusha was to accomplish was to bring Yahuah's Name back to its glory. Yahusha did not get killed by the Pharisees because he was healing people, he was hated by them because he was upsetting their earthly kingdom and control. The Pharisees ruled over the people with the authority to kill them for using The Name. And now this young man, the son of a carpenter was proclaiming all should now refer to the Alahim as Yahuah, the rightful Name.

The world continued to use the pagan name for Yahuah Alahim, even to this very day. Now is the time for the remnant to rise up and proclaim the correct Name of Yahuah Alahim so that it is restored to our lips. YashaYahu (Isaiah) 25:8–9 shows us what has happened and what is coming soon:

YashaYahu (Isaiah) 25:8–9

> *8 He shall swallow up death forever, and the Master Yahuah shall wipe away tears from all faces and take away the reproach of His people from all the areas (earth). For Yahuah has spoken.*
>
> *9 And it shall be said in that day, 'See, this is our Alahim. We have waited for Him, and He saves us. This is Yahuah, we have waited for Him, let us be glad and rejoice in His deliverance.'*
>
> YASHAYAHU 25:8–9 BYNV

Please note the Scripture is talking of Yahuah and Yahusha. Something to remember as we move forward in our letters. In closing I want to share with you a warning from

2Timothy 4:1–5.

> *In the sight of Yahuah and the Master Yahusha Mashiak (the Christ), who shall judge the living and the dead at His appearing and His reign, I earnestly charge you:*

Proclaim the Word! Be urgent in season, out of season.
Correct, warn, appeal, with all patience and teaching.
For there shall be a time when they shall not bear sound
teaching, but according to their own desires, they shall
heap up for themselves teachers tickling the ear, and they
shall indeed turn their ears away from the Truth and
be turned aside to myths. But you be sober in all things,
suffer hardships, do the work of an evangelist, accomplish
your service completely.

2TIMOTHY 4:1–5. BYNV

Modern day myths are things like: sacraments, holy water, beads/ rosaries, trinities, celibacy, image worship, steeples, chants, prayers to the dead and the list goes on.[1]

Teachers have been tickling our ears for centuries, and their lies have been accepted as truth. Until you know The Name you cannot see what is not truth. Sinners do not see what they are doing is sin.

I encourage you to remove the false names from your lips and speak the true Name; Yahuah and Yahusha. Many people find when they begin to use the correct names the Scripture of Truth begins to open up to them in ways they have not experienced before. They find they want to explore the Scripture of Truth and learn. They find they lose interest in the celebrations of man and move toward celebrating the feast which were instituted by Yahuah for His people. And although we cannot yet see it, we have His mark on us so that the reapers will pass over us when the tares are removed before the coming of Yahusha Mashiak.

Now that you know the Name and some of the history of what has happened. I encourage you to get your own copy of BYNV Scripture

1   You can find a more detailed list in Lew White's book "I AM YAHUAH, THAT IS MY NAME" on page 63. This book is available on www.TorahZone.net

of Truth. It is available on www.TorahZone.net in both a leather type binding and paper bound. It is also available on Amazon's Kindle Unlimited. I started with the Kindle Unlimited copy and quickly purchased the paper copy. I just love this Scripture of Truth.

For Yahusha's Joy,
A Natsari

30

LETTER PACKAGE 2:
THE GIFT OF THE SHABATH

LETTER 1:
WHO–WHEN–WHERE

*In this letter we will discover who
established the Shabath. When the Shabath
takes place and why it was created.*

*Greetings From: A Natsari, Follower of Yahusha
To You: Discovering the Way of the Natsarim*

First let's look at our Scripture:

Barashith (Genesis)2:1–2

> 1 *Thus the shamayim and the arets were completed, and
> all their array.*
> 2 *And on the 7th yom Alahim halted His work which He
> had done, and He rested on the seventh yom from all His
> work which He had made.*
>
> BARASHITH (GENESIS)2:1–2 BYNV

Right in the very beginning of Barashith (Genesis) we learn that
Yahuah was the one who created everything. He worked on His
creation for 6 days. He saw that his creation was good. Yahuah
decided he would rest on the 7th day. This 7th day of creation week
was the 1st Shabath; the first of His Appointed Times.

HONOR: High Respect, Great Esteem

Think about the work of creation that Yahuah did. He created everything. His work has immeasurable value for all eternity, and He took a day to rest. Yahuah knows His own value and his work but He did not need prove it by continuing to work non-stop. He created and took the Shabath Rest. He made that Shabath Rest an Appointed Time for his people, for all people. To me, that says, I am valuable to Yahuah and he wants me to take a day of rest with Him. I am delighted to honor Yahuah by keeping the Shabath.

Yahuah established the Shabath within the creation of all things. The Shabath will stand for eternity. No one will ever stop it because Yahuah has set it in place.

When Yahuah set the Sabbath in place He also set the number of days of the week in place. "Six days you will work and on the 7th day you will rest from your work." Yahuah makes this perfectly clear to the Israelites in the following scriptures. Yahuah only named the 7th day: Shabath of Yahuah.

Dabarim — (Deuteronomy) 5:12–15

12 Guard yom Sabbath, to set it apart, as Yahuah your Alahim commanded you

13 Six Yomin you labor, and shall do all your work,

14 But the seventh yom is the Shabath of Yahuah your Alahim. You do not do any work — you, nor your son, nor your daughter, nor your male servant, nor your female servant, nor your ox, nor your donkey, nor any of your cattle, nor your stranger who is within your gates, so that your male servant and your female servant rests as you do.

15 And you shall remember that you were a slave in the land of Mitsrayim, and that Yahuah your Alahim brought you out from there by a strong hand and by an outstretched arm. Therefore Yahuah, your Alahim commanded you to observe yom Shabath.

DABARIM — (DEUTERONOMY) 5:12–15 BYNV

Shemoth (Exodus) 31:13–17

To Mosheh:

13 And you, speak to the children of **Yisharal,** *saying, My Shabaths you are to guard, by all means, for it is a sign between Me and you throughout your generations, to know that I , Yahuah, am setting you apart.*

14 And you shall guard the Shabath, for it is set-apart to you. Everyone who profanes it will certainly be put to death, for anyone who does work on it, that being shall be cut off from among his people.

15 Six Yomin work is done, and on the 7th is a Shabath of rest, set-apart to Yahuah. Everyone doing work on the yom Shabath shall certainly be put to death.

16 And the Children of Yisharal shall guard the Shabath, to observe the Shabath throughout their generations as an everlasting covenant.

17 Between Me and the children of Yisharal it is a sign forever. For in 6 Yomin Yahuah made the shamayim and the arets, and on the 7th yom He rested and was refreshed.

SHEMOTH (EXODUS) 31:13–17 BYNV

Yahuah extended His Day of Rest and fellowship to his people — to all people — so that they could rest from their work and fellowship with Him. This is the purpose of the Shabath on the 7th day of the week.

There can be no argument with the seventh day of the week being the Day of Rest; the day Yahuah called Shabath to Yahuah.

Shane Willard explains living the Shabath this way: "The Sabbath is a day where you live like your work is done, even if it isn't — and that is healing. The world goes on, because Yahuah is Yahuah, and you are not. The supply of everything I need, is as close to me as the air that I'm breathing, I just need to stop and become aware of that."
Shane Willard, Ten Commandments,
Foundations for Success

The Sabbath was established during Creation when Yahuah had completed his work. He took time to rest and enjoy what he had done. We also need to learn to stop from our labors and enjoy what we have accomplished, spending time with Yahuah and our families. All people are invited to partake of the Sabbath. We learned that Mosheh was told this in Barashith 2:1–2. Mosheh taught the Israelites this in Dabarim 5:12–15 and Shemoth 31:13–17.

In our next letter, we will see the importance of the Sabbath and what we are acknowledging when we keep the Sabbath.

For Yahusha's Joy,
A Natsari

LETTER 2:
THE SIGN

*In our last letter, we learned: The Shabath was
established during Creation when Yahuah had
completed his work. He took time to rest and
enjoy what he had done.*

Greetings From: A Natsari, Follower of Yahusha
To You: Discovering the Way of the Natsarim

In this letter we will begin to understand the importance of the
Shabath and how it is THE SIGN between Yahuah and His people

Yekezqal (Ezekiel) 20:11–12

> *11 And I gave them My laws and showed them My right-*
> *rulings, 'which, if a man does, he shall live by them.'*
>
> *12 And I also gave them My Shabaths, to be a sign*
> *between them and Me, to know that I am Yahuah who*
> *sets them apart.*
>
> YEKEZQAL (EZEKIEL) 20:11–12 BYNV

In the scripture we find that Yahuah gave his laws and right rulings
to his people as they were making their way in the desert to the
promised land. He gave the laws and right-rulings because he was

trying to change the culture of a people group who had lived in slavery for 430 years. But beyond the laws and right-rulings He wanted something more. He loved his bride.

He wanted relationship with his people; the ones he had chosen to be his bride. He gave them the beautiful gift of His Shabath. An ongoing gift, not a one time gift, a gift for them and the generations that would follow them. A gift that would allow them to spend uninterrupted time with Him. They would have His total attention, if they came into Yahuah's Shabath.

He gave them the command "To remember the Shabath." Which meant now they would rest on the 7th day. No one in their household was allowed to work. They were to rest, enjoy family and visit with Yahuah.

To help them learn the new behavior of honoring the Shabath, Yahuah did not give them manna on the Shabath but instead gave them provision for two days on the 6th day each week. Coming from a life of slavery, this day of rest was a beautiful gift. Their Alahim wanted to spend time with them. Nothing was expected of them except to spend time with Yahuah. Can there be any better-quality time then a whole day with Yahuah.

The gift of Shabath is wonderful but there was another purpose to Shabath.

The Shabath was unlike anything any other people group did. None of the pagan gods/goddess demanded a day of undivided attention. (how could they, as they were not and are not alive.)

The observance of the Shabath told all other people groups that the Alahim of the Israelites was indeed alive, and He treasured His people so much that he dedicated a day each week to the growth of their relationship. They shared a day together. All married couples should follow this example!

For Yahusha's Joy,
A Natsari

LETTER PACKAGE 3:
IMMERSION

LETTER 1:
INTRODUCTION
TO IMMERSION

This introduction will share with you my heart for immersion and show you the very first immersion recorded in Scripture.

Greetings From: A Natsari, Follower of Yahusha
To You: Discovering the Way of the Natsarim

We are now going to explore Immersion. You may know about a popular activity that is called baptism. Immersion may be different from the baptism you have been taught about.

Maybe you learned that you were sprinkled with holy water as an infant. If not that, then possibly dunked into the church baptismal pool during a service where someone proclaims a prayer over you while you hold your nose and down you go and back. And the congregation applauds. Now they claim you receive the Holy Spirit.

I have done both. I don't remember the first time. The second time was my choice but because the teaching was not complete truth, I went under and came back up the same as I was. I expected change within me. I was encouraged to study many different scholars approved by the Assembly of God Church organization. I was 40 years old then and I was happy to have found J E S U S and salvation. After years of man's teachings and following the traditions of Christianity, I was still searching to know that I know that I know I would obtain life eternal. I knew I had not yet received the truth I was seeking.

I hesitated to share this little piece of my journey because all the people I met along the way seemed to be really good folks not trying to deceive me in any way but that they themselves have also been deceived. Shatan deceived Eve, Nimrod and Constantine and that deception has come down through the centuries of mankind. Now the truth is being made known to all who will listen and receive.

I finally learned The Name and the truth about Immersion. I immersed myself, prayed myself, gave my complete self to Yahusha. And discovered what it is to be taught by His Ruach. The teaching takes time. Many of us fall back into depending on men to teach us. We have to learn to give time to Ruach Qodesh and it is so worth it. At the wonderful, youthful age of 66 I have discovered you are NEVER too old to search and NEVER too old to finally discover truth.

Immersion has deep roots in Scripture and a profound effect on your walk with Yahusha. In the next couple of letters, we will dive into those roots so that you get a clear picture of how important immersion is to Yahuah. It is not something you do lightly or because it is the 4th Sun-day of the month and it is on the program at your local church, or because of the church's expectation for membership.

It is personal! It is personally between you and Yahusha. It is the deepest commitment you will ever make.

Immersion will have the biggest impact on your walk with Yahusha. If you did not get it right the first time, then you need to do it again and get it right because the quality of your walk depends on you getting it right. It is ok to have witnesses, but you do your own immersion, it is your relationship with Yahusha that counts for you. It is great to have witnesses who will celebrate with you but you are the one immersing yourself in Yahusha.

Every step of the Narrow Path is incredibly important and when I write about each one, I think it is the most important. You may wonder which one is the most important. I believe we will each have a different answer but none of them become important in your life until you know The Name and have a personal relationship with Yahusha. When you immerse and give yourself completely to Yahusha, then His Ruach comes to you. Remember he said he had to leave so the Father would send the comforter, the Paraklita. When you study the Testimony of Yahusha you will discover that the One who was coming to you is the One who was leaving earth to return as Spirit and be Omnipresent which could not happen in human form. So yes, it is true, I am intense regarding immersion. I want you to learn the deep roots of immersion and we shall begin with creation.

Barashith 1:2B, 6–10

> *2b And the Ruach of Alahim was moving on the surface of the mayim (waters)*
>
> *6 And Alahim said, "Let space come to be in the midst of the mayim, and let it separate the mayim from the mayim.*
>
> *7 And Alahim Yahuah made space and separated the mayim which were under the space from the mayim which were above the space. And it was so.*
>
> *8 And Alahim called the space shamayim (heavens)*
>
> *9 and Alahim said, "Let the mayim under the shamayim be gathered together into one place, and let the dry land appear." And it was so,*

*10 And Alahim called the dry land arets," and the
collection of the mayim He called 'yamin.'*

BARASHITH 1:2B, 6–10 BYNV

In the opening chapter of Scripture, we learn that all of creation was called out of the waters. Ruach was moving on the surface of the mayim (waters) when Alahim spoke that a space come in the midst of the mayim. The mayim were above and below the space. He called for the shamayim (heavens) to be gathered together into one place and to let dry land appear, which he called arets.

We see here that creation was immersed in the waters and Alahim called them out. Immersion began with creation.

In the next teaching lesson, we will explore Noak and the Ark. I cannot help but wonder if Yahuah was wanting us to see the importance of immersion because, as you will read, He used very large volumes of water in the Old Testament when performing these different immersions.

*For Yahusha's Joy,
A Natsari*

LETTER 2:
NOAK'S OBEDIENCE

In the introduction letter we learned we are responsible for our own Immersion.

Greetings From: A Natsari, Follower of Yahusha
To You: Discovering the Way of the Natsarim

In this letter we will take a look at Noak's experience with Yahuah and the ark.

Barashith 6:1–8

> *1 And it came to be, when men began to increase on the face of the arets, and daughters were born to them,*
>
> *2 that the sons of Alahim saw the daughters of men, that they were good, and they took wives for themselves of all who they chose.*
>
> *3 And Yahuah said, 'My Ruach shall not strive with man forever in his going astray. He is flesh, and his Yomin shall be 120 years.'*
>
> *5 And Yahuah saw that the wickedness of man was great in the arets, and that every inclination of the thoughts of his heart was only evil continually.*

6 and Yahuah was sorry that He had made man on the arets, and He was grieved in His heart.

7 And Yahuah said, "I am going to wipe off man whom I have created from the face of the arets, both man and beast, creeping creature and birds of the shamayim, for I am sorry that I have made them."

8 But Noak found favor in the eyes of Yahuah.

BARASHITH 6:1–8 BYNV

Even though Yahuah was really done with all of man, He was still looking for one person who He could see Himself in. And Noak found favor. Yahuah saw something in Noak that was of Himself. While the rest of the arets was filled with violence, Yahuah saw one man and his family who He would make a way for as he destroyed the rest of mankind. Yahuah would start over with this man.

Barashith 6:13–18, 22

13 And Alahim said to Noak, "The end of all flesh has come before Me, for the arets is filled with violence through them. And see, I am going to destroy them from the arets.

14 Make yourself an ark of gopherwood.

17 And see, I Myself am bringing floodwaters on the arets, to destroy all flesh in which is the breath of life from under the shaman — all that is on the arets is to die.

18 And I shall establish my Covenant with you, and you shall come into the ark, you and your sons and your ashah and your sons' wives with you."

22 And Noak did according to all that Alahim commanded him, so he did.

BARASHITH 6:13–18, 22 BYNV

Barashith 7:1,12, 16,19, 22

1 And Yahuah said to Noak, "Come into the ark, you and all your household, because I have seen that you are righteous before Me in this generation."

12 And the rain was on the arets 40 (days)yomin and 40 (nights) lailah.

16 And those going in, male and female of all flesh, went in as Alahim had commanded him, and Yahuah shut him in.

19 And the mayim were exceedingly mighty on the arets, and all the high mountains under all the shamayim were covered.

22 All in whose nostrils was the breath of the spirit of life, all that was on the dry land, died.

BARASHITH 7:1,12, 16,19, 22 BYNV

We see that Noak was favored by Yahuah. Yahuah made a way that Noak and all who were with him were delivered from the trouble; the flooding. They were in the water but not destroyed by the water. Surely, they came out of this experience with a new respect and fear for Yahuah. A new understanding of who Yahuah is and ready to continue to obey him when they released from the ark.

That which was immersed in the water died. That which came out of the water, Noak and all who were with him, were surely made new by the experience.

Yahuah's promise

Barashith 8:1, 14–16, 20–22

1 And Alahim remembered Noak, and all the beasts and all the cattle that were with him in the ark. And Alahim made a wind to pass over the arets, and the mayim subsided.

14 and in the 2nd month, on the 27th yom of the month, the arets was dry.

15 And Alahim spoke to Noak, saying,

16 "Go out of the ark, you and your ashah and your sons and your son's wives with you.

20 Noak built an altar to Yahuah and took of every clean beast and of every clean bird and offered burnt offerings on the altar.

21 and Yahuah smelled a soothing fragrance, and Yahuah said in His heart, "Never again shall I curse the ground because of man, although the inclination of man's heart is evil from his youth, and never again smite all living creatures, as I have done,

22 as long as the arets remains, seedtime and harvest, and cold and heat, and winter and summer, and yom and lailah shall not cease."

BARASHITH 8:1, 14–16, 20–22 BYNV

Barashith 9:8–9, 11–13, 17

8 And Alahim spoke to Noak and to his sons with him saying,

9 "And I, see, I establish My covenant with you and your seed after you,

11 "And I shall establish My covenant with you, and never again is all flesh cut off by the mayim of the flood and never again is there a flood to destroy the arets."

12 And Alahim said, "This is the sign of the covenant which I make between Me and you, and every living creature that is with you, for all generations to come:

13 I shall set My rainbow in the cloud, and it shall be be for the sign of the covenant between Me and the arets.

17 And Alahim said to Noak, "This is the sign of the covenant which I have establish between Me and all flesh that is on the arets."

BARASHITH 9:8–9, 11–13, 17 BYNV

Let's look at what happened in these scriptures.

- **Judgement:** Yahuah judged man for his wicked behavior. Because of this judgement a punishment would take place.

- **Search:** Yahuah searched for one human in whom He saw Himself. He found Noak

- **Offered Deliverance:** Yahuah offered deliverance from the coming judgement to Noak. Noak would have to obey to receive that deliverance.

- **Obedience:** Noak was obedient to all that Yahuah said

- **Judgement carried out**: The flood came.

- **Justice completed, Yahuah remembered Noak:** Yahuah dried the earth and released Noak and family from ark.

- **Noak offered a burnt offering**

- **Yahuah received the offering**
- **Yahuah gave a sign of covenant:** Yahuah made the rainbow in the clouds the sign of his covenant, reminding Himself, He would never destroy the earth by flooding again.

The flood destroyed all that was wicked. When the earth reappeared and dried out from the flood new life began again both with nature and with man. Noak and his family were brought up out of the water to begin mankind again. The key here is obedience. Immersion includes obedience.

Here is a review Yahuah and Noak's actions.

Actions by Yahuah:

- Judgement
- Search
- Offer of Deliverance
- Carried out Judgement
- Acted on the completed Justice by releasing Noak from the ark
- Yahuah received Noak's offering
- Yahuah gave a convenant sign to man the rainbow

Actions by Noak:

- Believed
- Obedient
- Burnt Offering
- Noak and family began to populate the earth again.

In our next letter, we will explore Abrahim, Circumcision and the Covenant. We will begin to understand how circumcision is attached to immersion in Yahusha.

For Yahusha's Joy,
A Natsari

LETTER 3:
ABRAHIM – CIRCUMCISION

*In our last letter, we learned how Noak's
immersion into obedience was credited to
him as righteousness.*

Greetings From: A Natsari, Follower of Yahusha
To You: Discovering the Way of the Natsarim

In this letter we will take a look at Abram's obedience and circumcision before the promised child could come forth.

The genealogy of Shem, son of Noak brought forth Abram. Now we will look at the covenant that Yahuah made with Abram and while it is not an immersion, it does show us the sign of the covenant that would have a continuing impact in understanding immersion today.

Barashith 12:1–3

> *1 And Yahuah said to Abram, "Go yourself out of your
> land, from your relatives and from your father's house, to
> a land which I show you.*
>
> *2 "And I shall make you a great nation, and bless you and
> make your name great, and you shall be a blessing!*

*3 "And I shall bless those who bless you and curse him
who curses you. And in you all the clans of the Arets shall
be blessed."*

BARASHITH 12:1–3 BYNV

Yahuah has just made a promise to Abram. Abram was 75 when he left his father's house and land. He took Lot with him. After Lot had **separated** from Abram, Yahuah revealed additional details of His promise. It would take 25 years before an important part of the promise would be realized. The promise: "I shall make you a great nation."

Barashith 13:14–16

*14 and after Lot had separated from him Yahuah said to
Abram, "Now lift up your eyes and look from the place
where you are, northward and southward and eastward
and westward,*

*15 for all the land which you see I shall give to you and
your seed forever.*

*16 And I shall make your seed as the dust of the arets, so
that, if a man could count the dust of the arets, then your
seed also could be counted.*

BARASHITH 13:14–16 BYNV

Yahuah confirms his promise to Abram however Abram did not yet have a son. While he could not see the promise being fulfilled and he was growing older he still believed and obeyed.

Barashith 15

1 After these events the Word (Yahusha) of Yahuah came to Abram in a vision, saying, "Do not be afraid, Abram. I am your shield; your reward is exceedingly great."

2 And Abram said, "Master Yahuah, what would you give me, seeing I go childless, and the heir of my house is Aliezer of Damascus?"

3. And Abram said, "See you have given me no seed, and see, one born in my house is my heir!"

4 And see, the Word of Yahuah came to him, saying, "This one is not your heir, but he who comes from your own body is your heir."

5 And He brought him outside and said, "Look now toward the shamayim, and count the stars if you are able to count them." And He said to him, "So are your seed."

6 And he believed in Yahuah and He reckoned it to him for righteousness.

...

13 And He said to Abram, "Know for certain that your seed are to be sojourners in a land that is not theirs, and shall serve them, and they shall afflict them 400 years.

14 "But the nation whom they serve I am going to judge, and afterward let them come out with great possessions.

15 Now as for you, you are to go to your fathers in peace, you are to be buried at a good old age.

...

18 On the same yom Yahuah made a covenant with Abram, saying, "I have given this land to your seed,

from the river of Mitsrayim to the great river, the River
Euphrates...

BARASHITH 15:1–6, 13–15,18 BYNV

Abram obeyed Yahuah because he believed in Yahuah. Very
important point for immersion. You have to believe in Yahusha
before you will obey Yahusha. Yahuah's promise to Abram is reaf-
firmed and Yahuah expands on the details of the promise, the inheritance of the nations to come that would come out of Mitsrayim with
great possessions.

Barashith 17:1–7

> *1 And it came to be when Abram was 99 years old, that*
> *Yahuah appeared to Abram and said to him, "I am Al*
> *Shaddai — walk before Me and be perfect.*
>
> *2 And I give My covenant between Me and you, and shall*
> *greatly increase you."*
>
> *3 And Abram fell on his face, and Alahim spoke with him,*
> *saying,*
>
> *4 "As for Me, look, My covenant is with you and you shall*
> *become a father of many nations.*
>
> *5 "And no longer is your name called Abram, but your*
> *name shall be Abrahim , because I shall make you a*
> *father of many nations.*
>
> *6 "And I shall make you bear fruit exceedingly, and make*
> *nations of you, and sovereigns shall come from you.*
>
> *7 "And I shall establish My covenant between Me and*
> *you and your seed after you in their generations, for an*
> *everlasting covenant, to be Alahim to you and your seed*
> *after you."*

BARASHITH 17:1–7 BYNV

Barashith 9–14

> *9 And Alahim said to Abrahim, "As for you, guard my Covenant, you and your seed after you throughout their generations.*
>
> *10* **This is My covenant which you guard between Me and you, and your seed after you: Every male child among you is to be circumcised.**
>
> *12 "And a son of 8 Yomin is circumcised by you, every male child in your generations, he who is bought with silver from any foreigner who is not of your seed.*
>
> *13 "He who is born in your house, and he who is bought with your silver, has to be circumcised. So shall My covenant be in your flesh, for an everlasting covenant.*
>
> *14 "And an uncircumcised male child, who is not circumcised in the flesh of his foreskin, his life shall be cut off from his people — he has broken My covenant."*
>
> BARASHITH 9–14, BYNV

Barashith 17:22–24

> *22 And when He had ended speaking with him, Alahim went up from Abrahim.*
>
> *23 And Abrahim took Yishmaal his son, (by Hagar, Sarah's servant) and all those born in his house and all those bought with his silver, every male among the men of Abrahim's house, and circumcised the flesh of their foreskins that same yom, as Alahim told him.*
>
> *24 And Abrahim was 99 years old when he was circumcised in the flesh of his foreskin.*
>
> BARASHITH 17:22–24 BYNV

Yahuah changed Abram. He changed his life and his future. This change is proclaimed by changing Abram's name to Abrahim. It was an outward sign. You are changed through immersion. Your life is changed and so is your future. You will display an outward change in your life after your immersion.

Obedience and Circumcision are signs of the Covenant

And so it was, Yahuah gave an expanding promise to Abrahim but that promise demanded obedience. Obedience was a sign of this covenant by Abrahim and his descendants in that they subject themselves to the circumcisions.

The sign of the covenant is that every male among Abrahim's people would be circumcised. Yahuah's covenant would be in their flesh, for an everlasting covenant, Barashith 17:13

Circumcision and Immersion are both covenant signs between you and Yahusha. Circumcision was an outward sign, but since Yahusha came our hearts are circumcised and the outward sign is the immersion into water. Our behavior and how we live our life are signs to the world we are different. We will continue to explore this subject as you make the decision for immersion and circumcision in the new covenant.

Dabarim 30:6

> *6 And Yahuah your Alahim shall circumcise your heart and the heart of your seed, to love Yahuah your Alahim with all your heart and with all your being, so that you might live.*

DABAARIM 30:6 BYNV

In the last three letters we have seen Yahuah reveal separation, obedience and circumcision. In creation He showed us separation. He separated the waters and produced land. With Noak He shows us obedience that produced righteousness and he separated Noak from evil by once again covering the land with water. In this letter Abrahim separated from Lot and all the males in his household were circumcised and then the promised child was conceived and born. This pattern of separation, obedience and circumcision will continue in the next three lessons. I want you to see this patten because true immersion demands separation, obedience and heart circumcision.

For Yahusha's Joy,
A Natsar

LETTER 4:
MOSHEH – SEPARATION CAN BE DIFFICULT

In our last 3 letters we learned about separation, obedience and circumcision. Now we begin the cycle again as we make our way to modern day Immersion.

Greetings From: A Natsari, Follower of Yahusha
To You: Discovering the Way of the Natsarim

Yahuah decides it is time for His chosen people to be set free from captivity. His plan for their freedom began with a baby born to a man from the House of Lui and the daughter of Lui. Scripture tells the story:

Shemoth 2:1–6, 9, 10

> *1 And a man of the house of Lui went and married a daughter of Lui.*
>
> *2 And the ashah conceived and bore a son. And she saw that he was a lovely child, and she hid him three months.*
>
> *3 And when she could hide him no longer, she took an ark of wicker for him, and coated with tar and pitch, and put*

the child in it, and laid it in the reeds by the edge of the river.

4 And his sister stood at a distance, to know what would be done to him

5 And the daughter of Faroah came down to wash herself at the river, and her young women were walking by the riverside. And when she saw the ark among the reeds, she sent her female servant to get it,

6 and opened it and saw the child, and see, the baby wept. So, she had compassion on him, and said, "this is one of the children of the Hebrews…"

9 And Faraoh's daughter said to her, "Take this child away and nurse him for me, then I shall pay your wages." So, the ashah (Mosheh's birth mother) took the child and nursed him.

10 And the child grew, and she brought him to Faraoh's daughter, and he became her son. And she called his name Mosheh, saying, "Because I have drawn him out of water."

SHEMOTH 2:1–6, 9, 10 BYNV

Yahuah created the arets out of the waters and now Mosheh was named for being drawn out of water. Mosheh was preserved in an ark by his mother and separated from the water by Faraoh's daughter. What was to come was that Yahuah would draw his people out through the sea because of the obedience of Mosheh who had been drawn out of the water. Water would have a special role in Yahuah's relationship with His people.

Mosheh grew up in the house of Faraoh. Events happened and Mosheh fled Mitsrayim and found himself in the household of the

Priest of Midyan. Mosheh agreed to dwell with them. The man gave Mosheh his daughter, Tsipporah as wife.

Shemoth 2:23–25

> *23 And it came to be after these many Yomin that the sovereign of Mitsrayim died. And the children of Yisharal groaned because of the slavery, and they cried out. And their cry came up to Alahim because of the slavery.*
>
> *24 And Alahim heard their groaning, and Alahim remembered His covenant with Abrahim, with Yitshaq, and with YaAqob.*
>
> *25 And Alahim looked on the children of Yisharal, and Alahim knew!*
>
> SHEMOTH 2:23–25 BYNV

Meanwhile Mosheh was shepherding the flock of Yithro his father-in-law, the priest of Midyan.

Shemoth 3:1b-5, 9–10

> *1b And he led the flock to the back of the wilderness, and came to Koreb, the mountain of Alahim.*
>
> *2 And the Messenger of Yahuah appeared to him in a flame of fire from the midst of a bush. And he looked and saw the bush burning with fire, but the bush was not consumed.*
>
> *3 And Mosheh said, "Let me turn aside now, and see this great sight, why the bush does not burn."*

*4 And Yahuah saw that he turned aside to see, and
Alahim called to him from the midst of the bush and said,
"Mosheh! Mosheh! And he said, "Here I am."*

*5 And He said, "do not come near here. Take your sandals
off your feet, for the place on which you are standing is
set-part ground."*

*9 And now, see, the cry of the children of Yisharal has
come to Me, and I have also seen the oppression with
which the Mitsrites press them.*

*10 "And now, come, I am sending you to Faraoh, to bring
My people, the children of Yisharal, out of Mitsrayim."*

SHEMOTH 3:1B-5, 9–10 BYNV

Many events happened which you can read in Shemoth. Faraoh
was not cooperative with Mosheh in letting the slaves go; at one-
point Yahuah said to Faraoh.

Shemoth 9:16

*16 And for this reason I have raised you up, in order to
show you My power, and in order to declare My Name in
all the arets.*

SHEMOTH 9:16 BYNV

It is important to see that Yahuah had always been in control of
all the events on the arets. Although Yisharal had suffered slavery,
Yahuah took what was meant for harm and reversed it with His
power and His Name.

After many signs and wonders Faraoh was still holding the Yisharal slaves captive. Even after his people had suffered several plagues,

Faraoh's heart was hardened so that the power of Yahuah was shown to all the people. Faraoh said to Mosheh:

Shemoth 10:28–29

> *28 And Faraoh said to him, "Get away from me! Watch yourself and see my face no more, for in the yom you see my face you die!"*
>
> *29 and Mosheh said, "You have spoken rightly — never again do I see your face!"*
>
> SHEMOTH 10:28–29 BYNV

Shemoth 11:1–7

> *1 And Yahuah said to Mosheh, "I am bringing yet one more plague on Faraoh and on Mitsrayim. After that he is going to let you go from here. When he lets you go, he shall drive you out from here altogether.*
>
> *2 Speak now in the hearing of the people, and let every man ask from his neighbor and every ashah from her neighbor, objects of silver and objects of gold."*
>
> *3. And Yahuah gave the people favor in the eyes of the Mitsrites. And the man Mosheh was very great in the land of Mitsrayim, in the eyes of Faraoh's servants and in the eyes of the people.*
>
> *4. And Mosheh said, "Thus said Yahuah, 'About midnight I am going out into the midst of Mitsrayim,*
>
> *5 and all the first-born in the land of Mitsrayim shall die, from the first-born of Faraoh who sits on his throne, even to the first-born of the female servant who is behind the handmill, and all the first-born of cattle.*

7 But against any of the children of Yisharal no dog shall move its tongue, against man or against beast, so that you know that Yahuah makes distinction between Mitsrayim and Yisharal."

SHEMOTH 11:1–7BYNV

Faraoh did not let the slaves go. And then Yahuah gave instruction to His people because Yahuah was going to carry out his judgement on Mitsrayim. Yahuah in carrying out this judgement, gains the honor and respect of the people. He showed Himself strong and caring toward his people. He proved to them He was able to deliver them from captivity.

Yahuah had made a covenant with Abrahim, He had confirmed that covenant with Yitshaq and YaAqob. Now Yahuah would deliver His people on the journey to fulfilling that covenant.

Yahuah instructed his people.

Shemoth 12:1–8, 11–14

1 And Yahuah spoke to Mosheh and to Aharon in the land of Mitsrayim, saying,

2 "This month is the beginning of months for you, it is the 1st month of the year for you.

3. "Speak to all the congregation of Yisharal, saying, 'On the 10th yom of this month each one of them is to take for himself a lamb, according to the house of his father, a lamb for a household.

6 'And you shall keep it until the 14th day of the same month.

7 And they shall take some of the blood and put it on the 2 doorposts and on the lintel of the houses where they eat it.

8 And they shall eat the flesh on that lailah, roasted in fire — with unleavened bread and with bitter herbs they shall eat it.

SHEMOTH 12:1–8 BYNV

Shemoth 12:11–14

11 And this is how you eat it: your loins girded, your sandals on your feet, and your staff in your hand. And you shall it in haste. It is the Passover of Yahuah

12 and I shall pass through the land of Mitsrayim on that lailah and shall smite all the first born in the land of Mitsrayim, both man and beast. And on all the mighty ones of Mitsrayim I shall execute judgement. I am Yahuah

13 And the blood shall be a sign for you on the houses where you are. And when I see the blood, I shall pass over you, and let the plague not come on you to destroy you when I smite the land of Mitsrayim.

14 And this yom shall become to you a remembrance. And you shall observe it as a festival to Yahuah throughout your generations — observe it as a festival, an everlasting law.

SHEMOTH 12:11–14 BYNV

Yahuah showed them how to use the Blood Covering to protect themselves during the execution of the judgement on Mitsrayim. Now we have these signs; separation, immersion, circumcision and blood. Yahuah has also introduced to Yisharal an appointed time, a festival, The Passover of Yahuah. We have a covenant made with Abrahim for him and his seed.

This is not a small thing you are considering immersing yourself into. Yahuah continues to reveal more about His plans for His people. He continues to show His people how Mighty He is and the depth of His love for His chosen people.

Now it is for you to grasp the importance of the Power of Yahuah and what He is able to do in your life. There is **no other like** Yahuah.

This judgement caused Faraoh to say to Mosheh:

Shemoth 12:13

> *13 Then he called for Mosheh and Aharon by lailah, and said, "Arise, go out from the midst of my people, both you and the children of Yisharal. And go, serve Yahuah as you have said.*
>
> SHEMOTH 12:13 BYNV

It was not long before the Mitsrites realized the Yahudim were not coming back and they had made a huge mistake letting go of their slaves. Faraoh called on all his finest 600 voice chariots with all his officers. All the chariots of Mitsrayim along with Faraoh's men pursued the Yisharal.

Sometimes separation is very hard and sometimes so slow you don't really realize what is happening. Yahuah is fully capable of walking with you through separation from your past. During my separation period, Yahuah slowly removed the ways of the world from me. Things like nightclubs, romance novels, movies, some music, desire to acquire unnecessary collection of things, "commercial" Christianity, and being tied to the behaviors of the masses. I did not recognize what was happening, I just lost interest in so many things and gained interest in Scripture. By the time complete separation came, it was natural. Yahuah will show you the way into your new life just as He did for me.

In the next letter, we will learn more about the difficulties of separation and the price for not separating when you have the invitation to do so. Not everyone accepts their invitation to separate unto Yahusha. You are exploring the narrow gate and path, which clearly says you have heard your invitation to Qodesh (to be set apart). Continue on the Path, embrace it. Your King awaits your acceptance of His invitation.

For Yahusha's Joy,
A Natsari

LETTER 5:
MOSHEH – IMMERSION INTO THE NAME

In our last letter, we learned Yahuah prepared from the birth of Mosheh to free, to separate His people from slavery.

Greetings From: A Natsari, Follower of Yahusha
To You: Discovering the Way of the Natsarim

In this letter we will see how Faraoh tried to hang onto his slaves and the people of Yahuah begin to get to know their Mighty One, Alahim.

Now the children of Yisharal took their flocks and herds. The Mitsrites urged the people to go so quickly so that they took their dough before it was leavened. They took the objects of gold and silver that Yahuah had instructed them to collect from their neighbors. They set out from Rameses to Sukkoth. There were about 600,000 men on foot besides the little ones.

Shemoth 12:38–40

> *38 And a mixed multitude went up with them too, also flocks and herds, very much livestock.*

40 and the sojourn of the children of Yisharal who lived in Mitsrayim was 430 years.

SHEMOTH 12:38–40 BYNV

Yahuah told the children of Yisharal that the Passover of Yahuah was to be remembered each year reminding them that the Torah of Yahuah is to be in their mouth. This became a law to them. This was to be an Appointed Time for them and all generations after them including the Natsarim today.

Shemoth 13:9–10,21

9 And it shall be as a sign to you on your hand and as a reminder between your eyes, that the Turah of Yahuah is to be in your mouth, for with a strong hand Yahuah has brought you out of Mitsrayim.

10 And you shall guard this law at its appointed time from year to year.

SHEMOTH 13:9–10 BYNV

21 And Yahuah went before them by yom in a column of cloud to lead the way, and by lailah in a column of fire to give them light, so as to go by yom and lailah.

SHEMOTH 13:21 BYNV

It was not long before the Mitsrites realized the Yahudim were not coming back and they had made a huge mistake letting their slaves go. Faraoh called all his finest 600 choice chariots along with all the chariots of Mitsrayim with officers on all of them and pursued the children of Yisharal. The chariots overtook them camping by the sea. The children of Yisharal cried out to Yahuah for they were scared.

Shemoth 14:13–14

> *13 Mosheh said to the people, "Do not be afraid. Stand*
> *still, and see the deliverance of Yahuah, which He does*
> *for you today for the Mitsrites who you see today, you are*
> *never, never to see again."*
>
> *14 "Yahuah does fight for you, and you keep still."*
>
> SHEMOTH 14:13–14 BYNV

Yahuah urged Mosheh to go forward by saying: "Mosheh lift up your rod and stretch out your hand over the sea and divide it, let the them go on dry ground through the midst of the sea." *They walked through the sea on dry land and they were under the cloud of Yahuah. This was an immersion. They were immersed in the Name of Yahuah as they walked on the dry sea bed as they were leaving behind slavery and crossing over to, immersing themselves in life with Yahuah which is freedom.*

The slavery they were leaving behind was that of Faraoh, which represents the adversary and the ways of the world in your life today. Yahuah took them out of all that, just as He wants to take you out of it today.

The column of cloud went from before them to behind them to separate Faraoh and his chariots from the children of Yisharal. All night Faraoh chased after Yisharal deep into the path of the sea. In the morning watch, Yahuah removed the wheels of the chariots and brought confusion on them. The Mitsrites realized they could not win against Yahuah and wanted to flee. Then Yahuah told Mosheh:

Shemoth 14:29–31

> *29 Then Yahuah said to Mosheh, "Stretch out your hand*
> *over the sea, and let the mayim come back upon the*
> *Mitsrites on their chariots, and on their horsemen.*

30 Thus Yahuah saved Yisharal that yom out of the hand of the Mitsrites, and Yisharal saw the Mitsrites dead on the seashore.

31 And Yisharal saw the great work which Yahuah had done in Mitsrayim, and the people feared Yahuah, and believed Yahuah and His servant Mosheh.

SHEMOTH 14:29–31 BYNV

Yisharal Immersed in the Name of Yahuah

While they journeyed in the desert the congregation of the children of Yisharal had many experiences. Yahuah introduced them to the Shabath and the Appointed Times. They learned to depend on Yahuah. The Shabath taught them to rest for a full day. They learned disobedience came with a heavy price. In the third month after leaving Mitsrayim in the Wilderness of Sinai Yahuah told Mosheh to tell the people:

Shemoth 19:3–6

3 And Mosheh went up to Alahim and Yahuah called to him from the mountain, saying, "This is what you are to say to the house of YaAqob, and declare to the children of Yisharal:

4 "You have seen what I did to the Mitsrites, and how I bore you on eagles' wings and brought you to Myself.

5 'and now, if you diligently obey My voice, and shall guard my covenant, then you shall be My treasured possession above all the peoples — for all the arets is Mine

6 'and you shall be to Me a reign of priest and a set-apart nation.' SHEMOTH 19:3–6 BYNV

This is the beginning of the ketubah (essentially a marriage contract, not romantic, traditionally bluntly written, clarifying the legal terms of the marriage and serve as binding documents.) This was the first ketubah ever written. Yahuah is telling them He wants to make them a Treasured Possession but there were conditions. Would they accept?

After they had agreed to be His Treasured Possession, Yahuah gave Mosheh the full marriage covenant which we refer to as the 10 Commandments. If they did not keep the ketubah, there would be consequences. These commands are a ketubah; a marriage contract; a covenant. They learned the right-rulings of Yahuah.

In Shemoth 24 we read how Mosheh related the word of the covenant and the right-rulings to the people and the people agree to obey. Then they built and altar at the foot of the mountain and *offered burnt offerings and slaughtered peace slaughtering of bulls to Yahuah.*

Shemoth 24:6–12

> *6 And Mosheh took half the blood and put it in basins, and half the blood he sprinkled on the altar.*
>
> *7 and he took the Sefer (book) of the covenant and read in the hearing of the people. And they said, "All that Yahuah has spoken we shall do, and obey."*
>
> *8 And Mosheh took the blood and sprinkled it on the people, and said, "See, the blood of the covenant which Yahuah has made with you concerning all these Words."*
>
> SHEMOTH 24:6–8 BYNV

Shemoth 24:12

> *12 And Yahuah said to Mosheh, "Come up to Me on the*
> *mountain and be there, while I give you tablets of stone,*
> *and the Torah and the command which I have written, to*
> *teach them."*
>
> SHEMOTH 24:12 BYNV

This covenant was only the beginning of what the children of Yisharal would learn about their Mighty one, Yahuah. This covenant had been made with the descendants of Abrahim which would greatly shape the people of Yahuah. It is this covenant, this Torah (instruction) that is so important to us today as we make our way to immersion and circumcision of our hearts. This is the very covenant we are pledging to obey when we immerse in the water pledging ourselves to Yahusha. Understanding what you are doing when you immerse into Yahusha is very important. It is a serious matter.

So once again we see the blood being used to seal the covenant. Now we have 2 covenants sealed with blood, the Passover of Yahuah, the 10 Commands and Appointed times identified and the Shabath is a huge part of their lives now. *While they were traveling in the desert they did not circumcise their male children.* This is important to Yahuah and we will learn how He takes care of this problem before they enter the Promise Land. The descendants of Abrahim have experienced immersion. A lot has happened to the "Treasured Possession" in a short period of time. But things did not go as Yahuah would have preferred because the children of Yisharal would not put their slave behaviors behind them and fully devote themselves to Yahuah. Because of their disobedience they wandered in the desert for 40 years and did not possess the Promise Land. All of the original Yisharal died in the desert.

Just before Mosheh was to go to his rest, he would transfer the reigns to Yahusha (Joshua), his trusted assistant.

Separation, circumcision, blood sacrifice, appointed times and The Covenant would be revisited with the younger generation.

In the next letter, we will see how Yahusha (Joshua) obeying the directions of Yahuah, prepares the next generation for their opportunity with Yahuah.

For Yahusha's Joy,
A Natsari

*We will see the events in "Italic" and * will be repeated when Yahuah begins to work with Joshua (Yahusha), Mosheh's trusted assistant.*

LETTER 6:
JOSHUA (YAHUSHA) – THE NEXT GENERATION

In our last letter about Mosheh's experience in the desert we learned how a generation failed to receive the promise.

Greetings From: A Natsari, Follower of Yahusha
To You: Discovering the Way of the Natsarim

In the last letter, we learned how Mosheh lead the people out of Mitsrayim into the desert for a journey to the promise land. All did not go as well for them as it could have. The Yahudim were not able to completely leave their slave life behind them and cling to Yahuah. They continually fell back into their old ways. Mosheh patiently worked with them for 40 years but the generation that left Egypt never got Egypt out of their hearts. The price for not clinging to Yahuah and moving forward with Him caused them not to obtain the promise; the Promised Land. Bamidbar (Numbers) 32:11,12

Yahuah allowed that generation to die in the wilderness and looked to the next generation, the generation born in the desert, to receive the promise. Yahuah will always fulfill His promises although the intended recipient may not receive it if they do not meet the conditions.

Now we will see how Yahusha (Joshua) prepared the younger generation at the direction of Yahuah. The first day on the job Yahusha gets his marching orders.

Be strong and courageous, for you are to let this people inherit the land.

Obedience

Yahusha 1:1–3

> *1 And it came to be, after the death of Mosheh the servant of Yahuah, that Yahuah spoke to Yahusha son of Nun, the assistant of Mosheh, saying,*
>
> *2 "Mosheh, My servant is dead, so now, arise, pass over this Yarden, you and all this people, to the land which I am giving to them, to the children of Yisharal.*
>
> *3. Every place on which the sole of your foot treads I have given you, as I spoke to Mosheh.*
>
> YAHUSHA 1:1–3 BYNV

Yahusha 1:5–8

> *5 No man is going to stand before you all the Yomin of your life. As I was with Mosheh, so I am with you. I do not fail you nor forsake you.*
>
> *6 Be strong and courageous, for you are to let this people inherit the land which I swore to their fathers to give them.*
>
> *7 Only be strong and very courageous, to guard to do according to all the Truth which Mosheh My servant commanded you. Do not turn from it right or left, so that you act wisely wherever you go.*

8 do not let this Book of the Torah depart from your mouth, but you shall meditate on it yom and lailah, so that you guard to do according to all that is written in it. For then you shall make your way prosperous, and act wisely.

YAHUSHA 1:5–8 BYNV

The very first instructions from Yahuah to Yahusha (Joshua) is that Yahuah is with him, to be strong and very courageous, to LET this people inherit the land, to guard to do according to the Turah, as Mosheh commanded (taught) you and do not turn to the right or left.

Let is an interesting word in verse 6. Its definition is to give permission; to allow. The words strong and courageous are also in the verse connected to the word let. Strong is possessing physical strength. Courageous is mental or moral strength to face danger without fear.

You also have a "land" to subdue. You have to subdue the ways of the world in your life. To do that, you also must be strong and courageous. Just like Yahusha (Joshua) you have received the same all-inclusive marching orders when you immerse yourself in Yahusha Mashiak. Yahuah will let you gain your inheritance by guarding and doing the Torah and do not turn to the right or left. Along your path, will you have to lean on our Deliverer, Yahusha to enter into the Kingdom. Going through the narrow gate and walking the path is not a lazy endeavor.

Now we will see the steps Yahusha (Joshua) took to prepare the people to: LET this generation inherit the land. Watch for appointed times, separation, obedience, water immersion, circumcision and blood as their path into their new life takes shape.

Yahusha (Joshua)had already set his face to be obedient toward Yahuah. Now we see that the officers will be obedient toward Yahusha (Joshua).

Obedience toward Yahusha

Yahusha 1:10–11

10 And Yahusha commanded the officers of the people, saying,

11 "Pass through the midst of the camp and command the people, saying, 'Prepare food for yourselves, for within three Yomin you are passing over this Yarden, to go in to possess the land which Yahuah your Alahim is giving you to possess.'"

YAHUSHA 1:10–11 BYNV

Remember when the previous generation prepared to pass out of Egypt? Ref: Shemoth (Exodus) 12:1–50 It is happening again. The younger generation must prepare to pass over the Yarden.

While they prepared (vs11), Yahusha (Joshua) secretly sent out two men to survey the land. Mosheh also sent men to survey the land. The result was not good, but it would not be the same for this generation. They were ready! Egypt was not in them.

Belief, obedience, separation

The men met Rakab while scouting the land. Rakab told the men;

Yahusha 2:9

9 and she said to the men, "I know that Yahuah has given you the land, and that the fear of you has fallen on us, and that all the inhabitants of the land melt away because of you."

YAHUSHA 2:9 BYNV

Fear of Yahuah separated the children of Yisharal from the inhabitants of the land. The inhabitants saw that the children of Yisharal were different and the inhabitants feared their Mighty One.

Belief

Yahusha 2:23–24

> *23 then the two men returned and came down from the mountain, and passed over. And they came to Yahusha son of Nun, and related to him all that had befallen them.*
>
> *24 And they said to Yahusha, "Truly Yahuah has given all the land into our hands, and also, all the inhabitants of the land have melted away because of us."*
>
> YAHUSHA 2:23–24 BYNV

Yahusha led the people from Shittim to the Yarden. They stayed there 3 days before they passed over.

Obedience

Yahusha 3:3, 4B, 5–8, 11–13, 17

> *3 and they commanded the people, saying, "When you see the ark of the Covenant of Yahuah, your Alahim, and the priest, the Luim, bearing it, then you shall set out from your place and follow it.*
>
> *4b "Do not come near it, so that you know which way to go, for you have not passed over this way before."*
>
> *5 And Yahusha said to the people, "Set yourselves apart, for tomorrow Yahuah is doing wonders in your midst."*
> *(Ref: Shemoth (Exodus) 14:13)*

6 And Yahusha spoke to the priest, saying, "Take up the ark of the covenant and pass over before the people." So they took up the ark of the covenant and went before the people.

7 And Yahuah said to Yahusha, "This yom I begin to make you great before the eyes of all Yisharal, so that they know that I am with you as I was with Mosheh.

8 And you, command the priest who bear the ark of the covenant, saying, 'When you come to the edge of the water of the Yarden, stand inthe Yarden.'"

11 "See, the ark of the covenant of the Master of all the arets is passing over before you into the Yarden.

12 "And now, take for yourselves twelve men from the tribes of Yisharal, one man from every tribe.

13 "And it shall be, as soon as the soles of the feet of the priest who bear the ark of Yahuah, the Master of all the arets, come to rest in the mayim of the Yarden, that the mayim (water) of the Yarden are cut off, the mayim that comes down from upstream, and stand as a heap."

17 And the priests bearing the ark of the covenant of Yahuah stood firm on dry ground in the midst of the Yarden. And all Yisharal passed over on dry ground, until all the nation had completely passed over the Yarden.

YAHUSHA 3:3, 4B, 5–8, 11–13, 17 BYNV

Vs 7: shows Yahusha (Joshua) is set apart. Yahuah is giving an outward sign to the people that He is with Yahusha (Joshua). That Yahusha (Joshua) has been selected for this position and they should honor him in this position. We see this done again for our Deliverer,

Yahusha during His immersion when Yahuah says; He is well pleased with Him.

Remember Mosheh lead the people through the river on dry land. They were being chased by Egypt, a symbol of the world, because they were so tightly connected to the children of Yisharal. Egypt did not want to let go of them and really there was a part of the children of Yisharal who were equally connected to Egypt and in many ways did not want to leave. Change is scary because it is an unknown. Be brave, follow Yahusha Mashiak with all your being.

No one chased this generation because this generation was not so tightly entwined with Egypt. This generation led by Yahuah, experienced the wonders of Yahuah. They were able to pass through the waters unhindered. You too will leave the things of the world behind and pass through the water in your coming immersion. Just as the younger generation had seen the mistakes of their parents, your eyes have been opened to see the ways of the world. Now you are choosing to follow Yahusha Mashiak instead of the ways of the world.

Just like Abrahim and Mosheh, Yahusha (Joshua) heard and obeyed. His greatness is in his obedience because it reflected the will of Yahuah. This was recognized by the people. Our Deliverer, Yahusha was made great in the eyes of the Yahudim through His obedience to His Father.

Yahusha (Joshua) commanded 12 chosen men to pick up 12 stones from the Yarden bed. These stones would become a remembrance to future generations of when the mayim of the Yarden were cut off before the ark, allowing the children of Yisharal to pass over on dry land.

Yahusha 4:10, 14

> *10 and the priests who bore the ark stood in the midst*
> *of the Yarden until every matter was finished that*

Yahuah had commanded Yahusha to speak to the people, according to all that Moheh had commanded Yahusha.

14 On that yom Yahuah made Yahusha great before the eyes of all Yisharal. And they feared him, as they had feared Mosheh, all the Yomin of his life.

YAHUSHA 4:10, 14 BYNV

This is what we refer to as a fore-shadow. This event was fore-shadowing something that would happen in the future. All of these events are for-shadowing the coming Deliverer.

Yahuah would confirm the greatness of our Deliverer, Yahusha in a river as he immersed Himself in obedience to His Father. This was done as an example for us of the importance of immersion and righteousness. Matithyahua (Matthew) 3:1–16

In this letter we have learned that belief, separation and obedience are all a part of our full immersion. We must believe Yahuah is able, we must separate ourselves from the world and we must want to be obedient to Yahusha.

In the next letter, we will learn how the Appointed Times relate to immersion.

For Yahusha's Joy,
A Natsari

LETTER 7:
JOSHUA (YAHUSHA) –
THE NEXT GENERATION 2

2 In our last letter how Yahusha (Joshua) lead the younger generation into the promise land and subdued the land.

Greetings From: A Natsari, Follower of Yahusha
To You: Discovering the Way of the Natsarim

In this letter we will see how in the midst of obtaining their promise they kept the Appointed Times, experienced immersion, circumcision and were commissioned.

Appointed times, immersion

Yahusha 4:19–24

> *19 And the people came up from the Yarden on the tenth yom of the first month, and they camped in Gilgal on the east border of Yericho*
>
> *20 And those twelve stones which they took out of the Yarden, Yahusha set up in Gilgal.*

21 And he said to the children of Yisharal, saying, "When your children ask their fathers in time to come, saying, 'What are these stones?'

22 Then you shall let your children know, saying, 'Yisharal passed over this Yarden on dry land,'

23 for Yahuah your Alahim dried up the mayim of the Yarden before you until you had passed over, as Yahuah your Alahim did to the Sea of Reeds, which He dried up before us until we had passed over,

24 so that all the peoples of the arets shall know the hand of Yahuah, that it is strong, so that you shall fear Yahuah your Alahim forever."

YAHUSHA 4:19–24 BYNV

Yahuah is repeating the parting of the waters type of immersion that He had done with their parents. He is taking them down the same path. Imagine what these folks are thinking. They are like you and they are a bit scared and excited. Their future was unknown. Actually, their immediate future of walking through the river bed was scary. They had to trust Yahuah was able to hold back the waters until they got to the other side.

It did not take long for all the sovereigns of the Kenanites, who were by the sea, to learn of this great deed Yahuah had done for the children of Yisharal. The hearts of the sovereigns melted and there was no spirit in them to cause any trouble for the children of Yisharal.

Circumcision, obedience

Yahuah demanded circumcision for the males of this younger generation after they had passed through the Yarden and the enemy: The Kenanites, were deep in fear and not going to attack.

Circumcision of the males was necessary because none had been circumcised during the 40 years in the desert. (Remember also that Abraham was not circumcised during his travels until it was time for the promise to be delivered.)

Yahusha 5:2, 4–6

> *2 At that time Yahuah said to Yahusha, "Make knives of flint for yourself, and circumcise the sons of Yisharal again the second time."*
>
> *4 And this is why Yahusha circumcised them: All the people who came out of Mitsrayim who were males, all the men of battle, had died in the wilderness on the way, after they had come out of Mitsrayim.*
>
> *5 For all the people who came out had been circumcised, but all the people who were born in the wilderness on the way as they came out of Mitsrayim had not been circumcised.*
>
> *6 for the children of Yisharal walked forty years in the wilderness, till all the nation — the men of battle who came out of Mitsrayim — were consumed, because they did not obey the voice of Yahuah...*
>
> YAHUSHA 5:2, 4–6 BYNV

After the men had been circumcised, they stayed in their places in the camp until they healed.

Today in immersion our hearts are circumcised. This is done by Ruach Qodesh in the moments of your immersion. He writes the Torah on your heart and makes your heart open to obey.

Romans 2:29

> *29 But a Yahudi is he who is so inwardly, and circumcision is that of the heart, in ruach, not literally, whose praise is not from men, but from Yahuah.*
>
> ROMANS 2:29 BYNV

Ephesians 4:19, 30

> *19 However, the solid foundation of Yahuah stands firm, having this seal, "Yahuah knows those who are His,"*
>
> *30 And do not grieve the Ruach ha'Qodesh of Yahuah, by whom you were sealed for the yom of redemption.*
>
> EPHESIANS 4:19, 30 BYNV

The children of Yisharal have been separated as the people of Yahuah which is evident by the Kenanites' fear of their Mighty One; Yahuah. They have passed through the Yarden and the males have been circumcised. Now it is time for the promise to be obtained.

Appointed times, separation

Yahusha 5:9–12

> *9 And Yahuah said to Yahusha, "Today I have rolled away the reproach of Mitsrayim from you."*
>
> *10 And the children of Yisharal camped in Gilgal and performed the Passover on the fourteenth yom of the month at evening on the desert plains of Jericho.*
>
> *11 And they ate the stored grain of the land on the morrow after the Passover, unleavened bread and roasted grain on this same yom.*

12 And the manna ceased on the yom after they had eaten the stored grain of the land.

YAHUSHA 5:9–12 BYNV

Yahuah washed the past off of the children of Yisharal. He washes your past off of you during your immersion and the circumcision of your heart. Your spirit is made alive and identifiable to Yahuah in that you are sealed for redemption. Your behavior, your lifestyle becomes your physical identity to the world that you are set-apart unto Yahuah. How you live or do not live the 10 commands speaks volumes about who you belong to.

Obedience, separation (set apart)

Remember when Mosheh saw the burning bush and Yahuah told him to take the sandals off his feet because he was standing on set-apart land. A similar event is about to happen again. Yahusha (Joshua) has a visit from the Captain of the host of Yahuah. Yahusha fell on his face to the earth and paid respect toward the Man.

Yahusha 5:14–15

14 "What is my Master saying to His servant?"

15 and the Captain of the host of Yahuah said to Yahusha, "Take your sandal off your foot, for the place where you stand is set-apart." And Yahusha did so.

YAHUSHA 5:14–15 BYNV

This event follows the belief, obedience, separation, crossing over, circumcision and the ending of one provision for a new provision. Now Yahusha (Joshua) is on set-apart ground. As you progress toward immersion you are believing, obedient, separated, crossing over, receiving circumcision of the heart and letting go of the world's provision for Yahuah's provision. Your life is about to reflect standing on holy ground.

Offerings and praise

In Yahusha 8 we read of a battle with sovereign of Ai. Yahuah had given Ai into the hands of the children of Yisharal. After the battle we read:

Yahusha 8:30–35

> *30 And Yahusha built an altar to Yahuah Alahim of Yisharal in Mount Eybal,*
>
> *31 as Mosheh the servant of Yahuah had commanded the children of Yisharal, as it is written in the book of the Turah of Mosheh, "an altar of unhewn stones over which no man has wielded iron." And they offered on it burnt offerings to Yahuah, and slaughtered peace offerings.*
>
> *32 And there in the presence of the children of Yisharal, he wrote on the stones a copy of the Turah of Mosheh, which he had written.*
>
> *33 And all Yisharal — the sojourner as well as the native — with their elders and officers and Rulers (Judges), stood on either side of the ark before the priests, the Luim, who bore the ark of the covenant of Yahuah. Half of them were in front of the Mount Gerizim and half of them in front to Mount Eybal, as Mosheh the servant of Yahuah and commanded before, that they should bless the people of Yisharal.*

34 And afterward he read all the words of the Turah, the blessings and the cursing, according to all that is written in the Book of the Turah.

35 There was not a word of all that Mosheh had commanded which Yahusha did not read before all the assemble of Yisharal, with the women, and the little ones, and the sojourners who accompanied them.

YAHUSHA 8:30–35 BYNV

The offerings were Thanksgiving. They were not sin offerings. The offerings were accompanied by the reading of the Torah, the blessing and the cursing. The Torah is for ALL People.

Both Mosheh and Yahusha (Joshua) read and wrote the Torah to the children of Yisharal, before going to their reward. I want you to see that the same thing is done for you.

Jeremiah 31:33

33 For this is the Covenant I shall make with the house of Yisharal after those Yomin, declares Yahuah: I shall put My Turah in their inward parts, and write it on their hearts. And I shall be their Alahim, and they shall be My People.

JEREMIAH 31:33 BYNV

Note in the passage above that the children of Yisharal and the sojourner as well as the native were ALL included. There is ONE Turah for ALL people.

I shall put My Turah in their inward parts
and write it on their hearts. And I shall be
their Alahim, and they shall be My People.

Commissioning of the people

When you read the book of Yahusha (Joshua) you will learn about their battles to subdue the promise land. Yahuah fought with them so they were able subdue the land. In Chapter 24, Yahusha (Joshua) does what Mosheh did at the end of his life. Yahusha gathered all the tribes to Shekem, called for the elders and for the heads and Rulers and their officers. He recounted their history. He reminded them of Yahuah's commitment to them and their commitment to Yahuah. And he said to them

Yahusha 24:14–15, 25–19

> *14 And now, fear Yahuah, serve Him in perfection and in truth, and put away the mighty ones which your fathers served beyond the River and in Mitsrayim, and serve Yahuah!*
>
> *15 And if it seems evil in your eyes to serve Yahuah, choose for yourselves this yom whom you are going to serve, whether the mighty ones which your fathers served that were beyond the River, or the mighty ones of the Amorites, in whose land you dwell. But I and my house, we serve Yahuah."*

And after these events it came to be that Yahusha, son of Nun, the servant of Yahuah, died 110 years old.

25 And Yahusha made a covenant with the people that yom, and laid on them a law and a right-ruling in Shekem

26 Then Yahusha wrote these words in the Book of the Turah of Alahim. And he took a large stone and set it up there under the oak that was by the set-apart place of Yahuah.

27 And Yahusha said to all the people, "See, this stone is a witness to us, for it has heard all the words of Yahuah which He spoke to us. And it shall be a witness against you, lest you lie against your Alahim."

28 Then Yahusha sent the people away, each to his own inheritance.

29 And after these events it came to be that Yahusha, son of Nun, the servant of Yahuah, died 110 years old.

YAHUSHA 24:14–15, 25–19 BYNV

I love this passage where it says, *Yahusha, a servant of Yahuah.* He had earned his place to be a servant of Yahuah. Before he was the servant of Mosheh, but by the end of his life he had risen to a servant of Yahuah. May we each rise to be the servant of Yahuah.

The accounts of Mosheh and Yahusha (Joshua) lives show all the components of immersion. The actual outward sign of going into, under and out of the water needs happens when you have completed some of these other experiences. Normally we do not look at all the experiences as being a part of immersion but without them you never get to true immersion.

You can go through the exercise of "baptism" without changing. Maybe you have. I know I did. I had to redo my immersion. It is ok to redo your immersion and get it right this time around.

We have spent quite a bit of time looking at the foreshadowing events in the Torah of what is immersion in the New Covenant. Each of these events are very important to Yahuah. He repeated them at least twice and I am sure with additional study we would find more.

In the next letter, we will take all these components into our New Covenant experience.

For Yahusha's Joy,
A Natsari

LETTER 8:
IMMERSION IN THE NAME OF YAHUSHA

In the Immersion letters, we have read about several immersion experiences in the Old Testament. Now it is time for Immersion in the Name of Yahusha.

Greetings From: A Natsari, Follower of Yahusha
To You: Discovering the Way of the Natsarim

In this letter you will find out how to complete your own Immersion into the Name of Yahusha

Wow, we have spent several letters learning about immersion in the first 5 books of scripture. The point was not to be repetitive even though Yahuah certainly repeated the process several times. The purpose is so you can develop a sense of the importance of immersion to Yahusha.

The important meaning of immersion for you right now is: to immerse into something is to completely enter into it. To cover yourself in something. To go deep. To give yourself to whatever it is you are immersing yourself into. In this situation to immerse yourself into Yahuah through the Name of Yahusha.

Maybe you were baptized before. Quite possibly under a different name then Yahusha. If that is the case, now is the time to immerse under the correct name. Possibly this is the first time you have learned about immersion. No matter where you have been or your present situation, if you want to immerse yourself in the Name of Yahusha, now is the time and place to do it. The following steps will help you.

In the previous lessons you may have picked up on the steps, but we will review them now.

- Believe
- Repent
- Immerse
- Outward sign and Circumcision of your Heart
- Make your pledge of good conscience toward Yahuah

Believe

You must believe Yahusha exists and that He died and was raised from the dead.

When Yahusha as an adult first comes to the public attention, He is walking toward his cousin, John the Baptist. John's Spirit recognizes the Spirit in Yahusha and says:

Yahukanon (John) 1:29–34

> *29 On the next yom Yahukanon saw Yahusha coming toward him, and said, "See, the Lamb of Alahim who takes away the sin of the world!"*

33 'Upon whom you see the Ruach coming down and remaining on Him, this is He who immerses in the Ruach ha'Qodesh.'

34 and I have seen and have witnessed that this is the Son of Alahim."

YAHUKANON (JOHN) 1:29–34 BYNV

This scripture tells us what Yahusha will do for us.

- Yahusha is the one who takes away the sin of the world
- Yahusha is the one who will immerse you in His Ruach ha'Qodesh (His Spirit)
- This will happen to you in your immersion.

Now you are ready to enter into His Covenant. In this covenant you are agreeing to a relationship with Yahusha. You are agreeing to obeying Him. His Covenant is a relationship. He created this covenant so that you can have life eternal with Him. You obey, He gives you life eternal. It is not about being a member of an organized religious group. This relationship with Yahusha is deeply personal and He is putting in you a love for His Torah.

Immersion is the moment you personally enter into the renewed Covenant with Yahusha and become a citizen of the Commonwealth of Yisrael. The moment He writes His Torah on your heart and enables you to love His Torah and obey His Torah. You now have received Eternal Life, the Life of the Son of Yahuah

Repent

Once you believe that Yahusha came to take away the sin of the World and that he will immerse you in his Ruach, it is time to repent.

Yahusha has done the work. The promise of forgiveness waits for you. To receive the promise you must take action. Now is time to recognize you are in sin and repent. Sin is any transgression against His Torah. You must determine in your heart to believe this.

1 John 3:4–5

> *4 Everyone doing sin also does lawlessness, and sin is lawlessness.*
>
> *5 and you know that He was manifested to take away our sins, and in Him there is no Sin.*
>
> 1 JOHN3:4–5 BYNV

The word "repent" means to turn away from sin and to go a different direction. In immersion we choose to turn back with all of our heart and we pledge to obey meaning to stop sinning.

Immerse

As you get in the water and begin to immerse yourself Yahusha is waiting for you. He is waiting for you to come to Him in repentance. Express your repentance to Him. Tell Him you know you are a sinner, that you are coming to him for deliverance, you believe in His cleansing Blood to wash away your sins. Tell Him you know that the penalty for your sin was laid upon Him and that by His death the penalty for your sins has been paid. Receive this precious gift Yahusha bought for you with His blood.

As you now go into the water completely, in your mind speak to Him, telling Him you believe that He died and was raised from the dead and now comes to live within you. That you know and believe He is piercing through the new soft heart He has created within you, bringing you His LIFE.

Immersion is your outward sign, if you have people around you to be witnesses that is great but if you don't do not worry, Yahusha is your witness. It is between you and Yahusha, you do not need an audience. People who know you will see the change in you without having seen your immersion.

Outward sign and circumcision of your heart

Immersion is Your outward sign of good conscience toward Yahuah.

Yirmeyahu 31:33

> *33 for this is the Covenant I shall make with the House of Yisharal after those Yomim, declares Yahuah: I shall put My Turah in their inward parts, and write it on their hearts. And I shall be their Alahim, and they shall be My people.*
>
> YIRMEYAHU 31:33 BYNV

This a beautiful verse. Yahuah wants you to be His and declares His desire in this scripture. Never doubt that Yahuah loves you and wants to be in relationship with you. Yahuah has a good conscience toward you.

The act of immersing is your outward sign of good conscience toward Yahuah. This means that with purpose you are going to listen to Yahusha and walk in His ways, keeping His Torah.

Kolossians 2:11–14

> *11 In Him you were also circumcised, in the putting off of the sinful nature, not with a circumcision done by the hands of men, but with the circumcision done by*

*Mashiach, 12 having been buried with Him in Immersion
and raised with him through your faith in the power of
Yahuah Who raised Him (Yahusha) from the dead.*

*13 And you, being dead in your trespasses and the
uncircumcision of our flesh, He has made alive together
with Him, having forgiven you all trespasses,*

*14 Having blotted–out the certificate of debt against us -by
the dogmas — which stood against us. And He has taken
it out of the way, having nailed to the stake.*

KOLOSSIANS 2:11–14 BYNV (certificate of debt — hand-
written list of accusations)

Make your pledge of good conscience toward Yahuah

1 Kefa 3:15–22 is scripture that defines the Pledge of a Good
Conscience toward Yahuah. After you come out of the water read
this scripture and imprint it deep into your being.

1 Kefa 3:15–22

*15 But set apart Yahuah Alahim in your hearts, and
always be ready to give an answer to everyone asking you
a reason concerning the expectation that is in you, with
meekness and fear,*

*16 having a good conscience, so that when they speak
against you as doers of evil, those who falsely accuse your
good behavior in Mashiak, shall be ashamed.*

*17 For it is better, if it is the desire of Alahim, to suffer for
doing good than for doing evil.*

18 Because even Mashiak once suffered for sins, the obedient for the unobedient, to bring you to Alahim, having been put to death indeed in flesh but made alive in the Ruach,

19 in which also He went and proclaimed to the Ruachs in prison,

20 who were disobedient at one time when the patience of Alahim waited in the Yomim of Noak, while the ark was being prepared, in which a few, that is, eight persons, were delivered through water,

21 which figure now also saves us: immersion — not a putting away of the filth of the flesh, but the pledge of a good conscience toward Alahim — through the resurrection of Yahusha Mashiak,

22 who, having gone into heaven, is at the right hand of Alahim, messengers and authorities and powers having been subjected to Him.

1 KEFA 3:15–22 BYNV

Now that you have completed your immersion you are living in His Covenant. As a member of the Renewed Covenant you are a member of the sect of the Natsarim, making you individually a Natsari. As a Natsari you are a member of the commonwealth of Yisrael. You are begotten from above, made new. His first coming accomplished the Atonement and now we wait for His second coming for the Redemption of Yisrael. You are awaiting birth at the second coming of Yahusha.

Neither you nor anyone else can improve on what Yahusha has done!

Always remember neither you nor anyone else can improve on what Yahusha has done. Once you have immersed you are done. According to Rev 12 & Rev 14 you are sealed in His Name. You are His and you obey the Commandments of Yahuah. As a Natsari you hold to the Testimony of Yahusha and guard his Name.

Lew White has an excellent article on Immersion. This lesson captures a lot of that article in a little different presentation. Take time to download and read the "Immersion" article which you will find: www.LambLegacyFoundation.com

Welcome to the Commonwealth of Yisrael.

For Yahusha's Joy,
A Natsari

LETTER 9:
JOSHUA / JESUS
VS
THE NAME, YAHUSHA

In this letter I want to address the use of the name Joshua and Jesus. Both men in Scripture carry the same name but it has not been presented that way in the Bibles.

In this letter we will address the English words Joshua and Jesus that are used in most all main stream Bibles. I had a problem with the translation of Mosheh's successor being called Joshua as well as a problem with the translation of Yahusha's name being Jesus. This letter will show you why both Joshua and Jesus are incorrect.

My 4th grade teacher use to tell me, when I was having difficulty understanding something, to just fill in the pigeon holes in my mind, as she ran her finger over my forehead, and it will all come together. We have some pigeon holes to fill in, but it will all come together. Okay, here we go.

Pigeon hole 1

The very first thing I want you to understand about these words is that the letter "J" was created around 1530 CE. Because the letter

"J" came into being around 1530 CE it is extremely clear and understandable that the letter "J" did not exist in the time of the original (Hebrew) Scripture of Truth. Under no circumstances would either of these men be called Jesus or Joshua.

Pigeon hole 2

Another point I want you to grasp is that the English language is made up of many foreign words. You speak Latin, German, Italian, Spanish and French as part of the English language without difficulty. At the time of writing this book, I lived in Tucson. We use Spanish names for many of our streets and we treat them as English words. The statement "I speak English, not Hebrew" is just not acceptable. We use foreign words in our everyday language all the time. As a matter of fact, when the word Jesus is used a person is actually speaking the Latinized form of the Greek, taken from IESOUS into the Latin Vulgate as IESU. "I speak English" does not hold up.

Pigeon hole 3

In the appendix there is a list of the Hebrew alefbeth. In English we have A, B, C etc. and we are taught their sounds. Hebrew letters actually have pictures and a name in addition for the "form" of the letter that go with them. For example, what we know as A, Hebrew presents as alef with an ox as the picture, B is Beth and a house is the picture. When looking at the Hebrew spelling you are looking at the name of the letter: Y = yod. Each letter has a certain sound. You can review the chart in the Appendix.

Pigeon hole 4

Another point I would like you to know regarding the Hebrew language is that Hebrew should be understood as the language (speech) of the man Eber. Yahuah's Word refers to Hebrew by the term Eberith. **Eber's name is applied to those descended from him (as an ethnic identification) as well as their script and language. Yahudah did not exist until later, however the tribal descendants and their language Yahudith stem from the man's name. The term Ebraidi (G1446) is transliterated (from Eberi) 11 times in the Natsarim Writings to describe the spoken language being used (see Acts22:2, 26:14).** Ref: http://www.fossilizedcustoms.com/hebrew.html

Acts 22:2

> *And when they heard that he spoke to them in the Hebrew language they kept greater silence.*
> ACTS 22:2 BYNV

Acts 26:14

> *And when we had fallen on the ground, I heard a voice speaking to me, and saying in the Hebrew language, 'Shaul, Shaul, why do you persecute Me? It is hard for you to kick against the goads.'*
> ACTS 26:14 BYNV

Pigeon hole 5

Next, I want to be sure you know the difference between Transliterations and Translations. Transliteration transfers the letters of a language to another, preserving the exact **sound** of the original language. Translation brings over a word's meaning to a new language. We are working with transliteration.

Transliteration: The sound of yod-hay-uau-**shin**-ayin is Ya-hoo-sha, Yahusha.

Translation: **There really is not a translation but the meaning of** yod-hay-uau-shin-hay is "I am your Deliverer."

Now just let all that information sit in your brain for a bit.

We are going to look at the original Hebrew of the two names, beginning with Mosheh's successor. His name is hay-uau-shin-ayin in Hebrew and we transliterate or get the sounds in the English letters Husha. Hay-uau = Hoo and shin-ayin = sha. shin-ayin is sounded out as sha which gives us Husha. The name Joshua is incorrect. Looking at the Hebrew it seems logical the translators should have use Husha. We also see Oshea in the KJV concordance.

Bamidbar 13:8

> *From the tribe of Afrayim: Husha, son of Nun.*
>
> BAMIDBAR 13:8 BYNV

Mosheh added yod- to his name = yod-hay-uau.

Now we have yod-hay-uau-shin-ayin

yod-hay-uau is sounded out as Ya-hoo and again shin-ayin is sounded out as sha which is Yahusha when we transliterate for the correct sound of the name in the English alphabet.

Bamidbar 13:16

> *And Mosheh called Husha the sone of Nun, Yahusha*
>
> BAMIDBAR 13:16 BYNV

Mosheh changed his successors name to Yahusha.

Pigeon hole 6

In the Greek Mosheh's successor's name is recorded as IESOUS.

When Yahuah came to be among his people, He selected a Name that described who He is and why He came.

Yahu — I am your
Sha — Deliverer

He named Himself, Yahusha; a description of who He is and What He was doing.

Pigeon hole #6 said the Greek name for Mosheh's successor is IESOUS. The Greek name for the Deliverer is also IESOUS. Both names are the same and they should be pronounced the same.

Translators chose to hide the true Name, following a tradition that began during the 70-year Babylonian Captivity of the House of Yahudah. The Pharisees made uttering The Name a stoning offense for anyone except the High Priest. The Pharsees controlled the doctrines during that time and approved Adonai (Lord) to be substituted when reading scripture aloud. The Pharsees did not like their authority being ignored by Yahusha and his followers. When Yahusha uttered The Name as he read the scripture, they picked up stones to kill him several times. What they did not know, but we do know is that Yahusha is The High Priest and had every right to utter The Name.

Over time translators followed the policy of using substitutions for Yahuah and completely had the wrong name for Yahusha.

However, one little detail in the Greek translation showing the name Mosheh gave Husha and Yahusha our Deliverer to have the same names preserved and confirms for us the correct Name for us today. Yahuah hide this revelation for us in plain sight and He told us to ask for the old paths where the way is good:

YirmeYahu 6:16

Thus said Yahuah, "Stand in the ways and see and ask for the old paths, where the good way is, and walk in it; and find rest for yourselves...

YIRMEYAHU 6:16 BYNV

The name of our Deliverer is Yahusha. The name Jesus is not a valid **name for our Deliverer** and was intentionally used to hide the true Name. The true Name has been revealed to you in these letters, if not before.

There is a lot more detail to back this up which I have not gone into however, you can read about this in two articles: The Real Name and Hebrew Phonology by Lew White. Both of these articles can be found on www.LambLegacyFoundation.com in the "Articles of Truth." Membership on the web site is free.

Words you think are of English origin!

Celtic = Dover, Cumberland, Thames, Avon, Trent, Severn (www.studyenglishtoday.net)

Norse = sky, egg, cake, skin, leg, window (wind eye) husband, fellow, skill, anger, flat, odd, ugly, get, give, take, raise, call, die, they, their, them (History of the English Language, Kryss Katsiavriades)

French = crown, castle, court, gown, beauty, banquet, art, poet, romance, duke, servant, peasant, traitor and governor ("Language Timeline", The British Library Board)

For Yahusha's Joy,
A Natsari

LETTER PACKAGE 4: TESTIMONY OF YAHUSHA

112

LETTER 1:
YAHUSHA – CHARACTER

*In this introduction to the Testimony of Yahusha
we will first look at some to the attributes of
Yahusha's understandings and behaviors*

*Greetings From: A Natsari, Follower of Yahusha
To You: Discovering the Way of the Natsarim*

The first thing I want to share with you are some scriptures that show us some of the characteristics of Yahusha.

Yahusha knew the Father's name

John 17:6

> *I have revealed your Name to the men whom you gave me out of the world. They were yours and you gave them to me, and they have guarded Your Word.*
>
> JOHN 17:6 BYNV

Yahusha knew Yahuah is One

Dabarim (Numbers)6:4–5

> *Hear O Yisharal: Yahuah our Alahim, Yahuah is ONE!*
>
> DABARIM 6:4–5 BYNV

Yahusha had ears to hear, to understand and to obey Yahuah

Matthew 13:9

> *He who has ears to hear, let Him hear.*
>
> MATTHEW 13:9 BYNV

Yahusha did not worry about his life, but in all things trusted Yahuah. He sought Yahuah at every turn (Scripture records how often he went off alone to be with the Father)

Matthew 6:31–33

> *31 Do not worry then saying "what shall we eat or what shall we drink or what shall we wear.*
>
> *32 For all these the Nations seek for. And your heavenly Father knows you need all these.*
>
> *33 But seek first the reign of Yahuah and his Uprightness, and all these matters shall be added to you.*
>
> MATTHEW 6:31–33 BYNV

Yahusha was obedient to Yahuah

Romans 6:16

> *16 Do you not know that to whom you present yourselves servants for obedience, you are servants of that one whom you obey, whether of sin to death or of obedience to righteousness.*
>
> ROMANS 6:16 BYNV

Yahusha humbled himself

Philippians 2:5–8

> *5 For, let this mind be in you which was also in Mashiak Yahusha,*
>
> *6 Who, being the essence of Yahuah, considered it not theft to be the same as Yahuah;*
>
> *7 yet emptied Himself, taking the form of a servant, and came to be in the likeness of men.*
>
> *8 And having been perceived in the form of a man, He humbled Himself and became obedient to death, death even of a Stake*

PHILIPPIANS 2:5–8 BYNV

Keeping the Testimony of Yahusha starts with knowing Yahusha and how he lived his life. We have just looked at some of those attributes. We want the same characteristics. We develop these characteristics by submitting ourselves completely to Yahusha in every aspect of our thinking, behavior, and actions.

As I give you the following modern-day analogy, please keep in mind Phil 2:5–8. Yahuah and Yahusha are one. We are looking at what Yahuah did as Yahusha our Redeemer.

You may remember a couple years ago, all the life/business coaches continually drill us on knowing our "why." Currently the hype is about knowing your "Story." As you set out to enter through the narrow gate and travel the narrow path, your love for Yahuah needs to be your driving force. You want your love for your Creator; Yahuah to be at the center of your "why." You want Yahusha's "story" of love for the Father and love toward your neighbor to be your "story." The Testimony of what people experience in you.

Yahusha loves Yahuah with all His being and heart. In the next lesson we will look at how Yahusha loved Yahuah with all his heart as a human. We want to do the same and to live as Yahusha lives.

For Yahusha's Joy,
A Natsari

LETTER 2:
YAHUSHA'S BEHAVIORS

In the last letter, we learned about the attributes of Yahusha so that we can work to obtain those same characteristics.

Greetings From: A Natsari, Follower of Yahusha
To You: Discovering the Way of the Natsarim

In this lesson we will explore some of Yahusha's behaviors that shaped his life. As we are his disciples we want to follow after Him so that His behaviors shape our lives. We want to capture how He expressed His love for The Father, Yahuah, so that we can do the same.

1 Yahukanon: 3–5

> *3 For this is the love for Yahuah, that we guard His commands, and His commands are not difficult, because everyone having been begotten of Yahuah overcomes the world. And this is the overcoming that has overcome the world: our belief. Who is the one who overcomes the world but he who believes that Yahusha is the Son of Yahuah?*

1 YAHUKANON:3–5 BYNV

Yahusha expressed His love for His Father by obeying the Torah. He was able to do this because he was begotten by Yahuah. When you complete your immersion you also are begotten by Yahuah enabling you to keep the Torah when you set your heart to do so. Overcoming the world is believing Yahusha is the Son of Yahuah regardless of peer pressure, media, religion and even your family beliefs. It will not always be easy, others will not understand but you understand, and you have to stay true to Yahusha.

Yahusha abandoned Himself to the will of the Father. He became a servant to His Father. As a human he abandoned all the desires of the flesh and bent Himself to the will and purpose of the Father. He did not allow His flesh to rule over his Spirit. There was no selfishness in him. Selfishness drives humans to do what they want to do for their own benefit with no regard for the will of the Father.

Yahusha became a servant to his Father Yahuah. In living out and guarding the Testimony of Yahusha we are to abandon ourselves, our flesh, to Yahusha. We are to abandon all the desires of the flesh and bend our will to the will of Yahuah. In doing the will of Yahuah you will be delighted with His attention toward you and his perfect gifts for you.

It was Yahuah's will for Yahusha to be immersed as an example for men. After his immersion The Ruach (Spirit) of Yahuah descended upon him and abode with him. The Ruach of Yahuah remained in Him.

Matithyahua (Matthew) 3:14–16

> 14 But Yahukanon was hindering Him, saying, "I need to be immersed by You, and You come to me?"

15 But Yahusha answering, said to him, "Allow it now, for thus it is fitting for us to fill all righteousness." Then he allowed Him.

16 And having been immersed, Yahusha went up immediately from the water, and see, the shamayim were opened, and He saw the Ruach of Alahim descending like a dove and coming upon Him,

17 and see, a voice out of the shamayim, saying, "This is My Son, the Beloved, In Whom I did delight."

MATITHYAHUA (MATTHEW) 3:14–16 BYNV

Yahusha's spirit is the Spirit of Yahuah. Yahusha was guided in all things by Ruach HaQodesh. We also are guided by the Ruach HaQodesh when we abandon our will to the will of Yahuah. Although, it may seem scary to let go of your desires and seek the desires of Yahuah, you need not fear because the Ruach HaQodesh will guide you every step of the way as long as you allow Him to guide you.

Yahusha's behaviors:

- Loves Yahuah through obeying the Torah
- Servant to Yahuah by abandoning His will to Yahuah's will
- Humble Himself to be guided by Ruach HaQodesh

All of these behaviors lead Yahusha to giving His life so that you may choose life everlasting. Eternal life with Yahusha is one of the gifts to you from Yahusha's life and sacrifice. Yahusha's gift restores you to the favor of Yahuah. Because of that favor you have been given as a counselor, The Ruach of Yahuah.

Yahusha's life is the example we strive to live. Life eternal with Yahusha is the amazing gift of His life and sacrifice which is available to us because Yahusha has returned us to favor with Yahuah.

Yahukanon 16:7

> *7 But I say the truth to you. It is better for you that I go*
> *away, for if I do not go away, the Paraklita shall not come*
> *to you at all, but if I go, I shall send Him to you.*

YAHUKANON 16:7 BYNV

Yahusha could not be omnipresent in his human body. He had
to leave so he could return to us in His Spirit form. Yahusha's Spirit;
Ruach HaQodesh is the one you may have been taught is the 3rd
person of a trinity. This is not a correct teaching. The Paraklita is the
Spirit of Yahusha. He did not send someone different or apart from
Himself. He returned to the Father so that He could come back to
us Omnipresent through His Spirit. He is in each one of His own,
enabling you to obey the Torah.

Review these behaviors and bring them into your life. In the next
letter, you will come to understand the Secret of the Testimony.

For Yahusha's Joy,
A Natsari

LETTER 3:
THE SECRET OF
YAHUSHA'S TESTIMONY

*In the last letter, we learned about the behaviors
of Yahusha. We also learned that Yahusha had
to return to The Father so that He could send His
Spirit to each of us. Greetings From: A Natsari,
Follower of Yahusha*

Greetings From: A Natsari, Follower of Yahusha
To You: Discovering the Way of the Natsarim

In this letter we will provide Scripture to reveal the secret, however
you will only fully accept the secret when the Spirit of Yahusha
places acceptance in your heart. Pray before you read for revelation of the secret.

To guard the testimony of Yahusha you have to know the secret of
the Testimony. To know the secret, you have to know who Yahusha
is. You need to know His identity.

You may know Yahusha is your Redeemer, which is correct but
there is more to understanding who He is. You may know He laid
down His life on the stake and of his own free will poured out his
blood as the final complete sacrifice so that you could have life

everlasting with Yahusha. He exchanged His blood so that you could have favor with Yahuah. Remember, under the old covenant, the priest sacrificed animals as the blood sacrifice but that is done away with because Yahusha completed the final sacrifice sealing the new covenant.

John 10:18

> *18 Because of this the Father loves Me, because I lay down My life, in order to receive it again. No one takes it from Me, but I lay it down of Myself. I have authority to lay it down, and I have authority to receive it again. This command I have received from My Father.*
>
> JOHN 10:18 BYNV

A mystery

There is more to capture in your heart about Yahusha. Let's uncover the secret of His Identity.

Matthew 13:27

> *27 All have been handed over to Me by My Father, and no one knows the Son except the Father. Nor does anyone know the Father except the Son, and he to whom the Son wishes to reveal Him."*
>
> MATTHEW 13:27 BYNV

In this scripture we are shown there is a mystery to solve. Who can solve this mystery? Only those to whom it has been revealed to by the Son. The answer to the mystery is in plain sight and recorded in the scripture.

The key to knowledge is hidden

Luke 11:52

> 52 "Woe to you experts in the law, because you have
> taken away the key to knowledge. You yourselves have not
> entered, and you have hindered those who were entering.
>
> LUKE 11:52 BYNV

Yashayahu 52:4–6

> 4 "For thus said the Master Yahuah, 'At first My people
> went down into Mitsrayim to sojourn there, and Ashshur
> oppressed them without cause.
>
> 5 And now, what have I here," declares Yahuah, 'that My
> people are taken away for naught? Those who rule over
> them make them wail,' says Yahuah, 'and My Name is
> despised all yom continually.'
>
> 6 'Therefore My people shall know My Name, in that yom,
> for I am the One Who is speaking. See, it is I.'
>
> YASHAYAHU 52:4–6 BYNV

Here we learn that Yahuah removed His Name from his people and
the experts of the time; the Pharisees, where the ones who carried
out that task. They replace The Name.

(*In the letters under The Name you learned how that was done and
why. This may be a good time to review those letters before proceeding.*)

When the Pharisees removed and replaced The Name, they took
away from the (common) people the Key to Knowledge. The Name
is the key of knowledge. Yahusha is telling you in Luke 11:52 that the
Pharisees had not used the Key to enter into understanding. Beyond

not entering themselves, they hide The Name and have kept all of us from receiving the key and entering into understanding.

What have they kept from us?

Daniel 12:3–4

> *3 "And those who have insight shall shine like the brightness of space, and those who lead many to righteousness like the stars forever and ever.*
>
> *4 But you, Danial, hide the words, and seal the book until the time of the end. Many shall diligently search, and knowledge shall increase."*
>
> DANIEL 12:3–4 BYNV

According to Daniel those who know the secret shall shine and this was to be hidden until the time of the end. They have kept us from being able to lead many to righteousness.

Using the key to open understanding

In the letters; The Name, you were able to learn The Name and received the Key but now we must use the key to open understanding.

Alahim's Name; Yahuah is the key of knowledge and will be sealed upon your forehead.

Revelation 7:2–3

> *2 And I saw another messenger coming up from the rising of the sun, holding the seal of the living Yahuah. And he cried with a loud voice to the four messengers to whom it was given to harm the arets and the sea,*

3 saying, "Do not harm the arets, nor the sea, nor the trees until we have sealed the servants of our Yahuah upon their foreheads."

REVELATION 7:2–3 BYNV

Who can heal? Who does Yahusha say He is?

Dabarim 32:39

39 See now the I, I am He, and there is no Alahim besides Me. I put to death and I make alive. I have wounded, and I heal. And from My hand no one delivers!

DABARIM 32:39 BYNV

Luke 4:17–21

17 And the scroll of the prophet YashaYahu was handed to Him. And having unrolled the scroll, He found the place where it was written:

18 The Ruach of Yahuah is upon Me, because He has anointed Me Alef-Tau

to bring the besorah to the poor. He has sent Me to heal the broken-hearted,

19 to proclaim release to the captives and recovery of sight to the blind, to send away crushed ones with a release, to proclaim the acceptable year of Yahuah."

20 And having rolled up the scroll, He gave it back to the attendant and sat down. The eyes of all in the congregation were fixed upon Him.

21 And He began to say to them, "Today this Scripture has been concluded in your hearing."

LUKE 4:17–21 BYNV

Luke 5:17b, 20–24

17 And the power of Yahuah was present to heal them.

20 And having seen their belief, He said to him, "Man, your sins are forgiven you."

21 And the scribes and the Pharisees began to reason, saying, "Who is this who speaks blasphemies? Who is able to forgive sins except Alahim alone?"

22 And Yahusha, knowing their thoughts, answering, said to them, "Why are you reasoning in your hearts?

23 Which is easier, to say, 'Your sins are forgiven you,' or to say, 'Rise up and walk'?

24 But in order for you to know that the Son of Adam possesses authority on arets to forgive sins..." He said to the man who was paralyzed, "I say to you, rise, take up your bed, and go to your house."

LUKE 5:17B, 20–24 BYNV

Yahusha had just read Isa 61:1 and proclaimed Himself to be the One the Scripture was speaking of. He is proclaiming Himself to be Alef-Tau, the beginning and the end.

Yahuah has said He is the one who does the healing and there is no other. In Luke 5, Yahusha not only confirms his authority to heal but also to forgive sin.

Yahuah

Revelation 4:8

> *Qodesh, Qodesh, Qodesh, Yahuah Al Shaddai, Who was*
> *and Who is and Who is coming.*
>
> REVELATION 4:8 BYNV

Do you see the secret? Is the Spirit of Yahusha revealing it to you?

The Redeemer, The Deliverer

YashaYahu 44:24

> 24 *"Thus said Yahuah, your Redeemer, and He Who*
> *formed you from the womb, 'I am Yahuah, doing all,*
> *stretching out the heavens all alone, spreading out the*
> *earth, with none beside Me…"*
>
> YASHAYAHU 44:24 BYNV

Husha 13:4

> 4 *But I am Yahuah your Alahim since the land of*
> *Mitsrayim, and an Alahim besides Me you shall not know,*
> *for there is no other Deliverer besides Me.*
>
> HUSHA 13:4 BYNV

1 Timothy 4:10

> 10 *It is for this that we labor and struggle, because we*
> *trust in the living Yahuah, who is the Deliverer of all men,*
> *particularly of those who believe.*
>
> 1 TIMOTHY 4:10 BYNV

Luke 2:11

> *11 Because ther was born to you today in the city of Daud*
> *a Deliverer, who is Mashiak, the Master.*
>
> LUKE 2:11 BYNV

In these Scriptures Yahuah says He is our Redeemer. Whose Name means, I am your Deliverer?

Do you see the Secret? Is the Spirit of Yahusha revealing it to you?

Open the eyes of your heart

YashYahu 45:6–7

> *6… so that they know from the rising of the sun to its*
> *setting that there is none but Me. I am Yahuah and there*
> *is none else,*
>
> *7 forming light and creating darkness, making peace and*
> *creating evil. I Yahuah, do all these.'*
>
> YASHYAHU 45:6–7 BYNV

Barashith 1:3,4

> *3 And Alahim said, "Let light come to be," and light came*
> *to be.*
>
> *4 And Alahim Alef-Tau saw the light, that it was good.*
> *And Alahim separated the light from darkness.*
>
> BARASHITH 1:3,4 BYNV

Kolossians 2:6 -10

> *6 Therefore, as you accepted Mashiak Yahusha the Master*
> *walk in Him,*

7 having been rooted and built up in Him and established in the belief, as you were taught, overflowing in it with thanksgiving

8 See to it that no one makes a prey of you through philosophy and empty deceit, according to the tradition of men, according to the elementary things of the world, and not according to Mashiak.

9 Because in Him dwells all the Fullness of Yahuah bodily,

10 and you have been made complete in Him, who is th Head of all principality and authority.

KOLOSSIANS 2:6–10 BYNV

Yahukanon 10:37–38

37 If I do not do the works of My Father, do not believe Me;

38 but if I do, though you do not believe Me, believe the works, so that you know and believe that the Father is in Me, and I in Him."

Yahukanon 12:45

45 And he who sees Me sees Him who sent Me.

YAHUKANON 10:37–38 BYNV

Yahukanon 17:11

11 And I am no more in the world, but these are in the world, and I come to You. Set-apart Father, guard them in Your Name which You have given Me, so that they might be one, as We are.

YAHUKANON 17:11 BYNV

In Yashayahu 45 Yahuah says besides Him there is none other, He is the only Alahim. Only He formed the light and created darkness. Barashith 1 says Alahim Alef-Tau saw the light, who claimed to be Alef-Tau in Luke4:17–21. Kolossians tells us the fullness of Yahuah dwells in Yahusha. Yahukanon tell us, if you don't believe Yahusha believe the works so that you can believe the Father is in Yahusha and goes on to ask Yahuah to guard us in His Name, so we might be one as Yahuah and Yahusha are one.

Do you see the secret? Has the Spirit of Yahusha revealed the secret to you?

A final thought

All of the quoted scriptures are showing you the secret. The testimony of Yahusha holds a secret that is revealed to those who are His. The secret is that Yahuah is Yahusha and Yahusha is Yahuah. They are one in the same. Yahuah came as, "I am your Deliverer", which in Hebrew is the name Yahusha. Yahuah came in the form of sinful man, but without sin and called Himself what He was doing. What was he doing? He was delivering us out of death. He came as our Deliverer. He came in the form of the man named Yahusha who is our Deliverer.

Pray that is secret will be revealed in your heart.

In *Beyond the Narrow Gate* we will look at your life going forward. Now that you have more understanding on what is expected of you as a follower of Yahusha you can help others to see the truth and begin their journey.

You have been Commissioned!

For Yahusha's Joy,
A Natsari

APPENDIX

Turah of Yahuah (Teaching of Yahuah)

1. I am Yahuah your Alahim, Have no other before My Face
2. You do not bow to images
3. You do not cast the Name of Yahuah your Alahim to ruin
4. Remember the Shabath, to keep it qodesh
5. You respect your father and your mother
6. You do not murder
7. You do not break wedlock
8. You do not steal
9. You do not bear false witness against your neighbor
10. You do not covet your neighbor's wife, house, field, servants, animals, or anything that belongs to your neighbor

Summed up in the whole body of this scripture: a new commandment:

1. LOVE ONE ANOTHER (Yahusha)

Who are the Natsarim?

Acts 24:5

5 For having found this man a plague, who stirs up dissension among all the Yahuim throughout the world, and a ringleader in the sect of the Natsarim,

ACTS 24:5 BYNV

Acts 28:22

22 "And we think it right to hear from you what you think, for indeed concerning this sect, we know that it is spoken against everywhere."

ACTS 28:22 BYNV

Natsarim the first fruits. We are those who do 2 things: We obey the Turah, Commands of Yahuah, and hold to the Testimony of Yahusha. We are guardians or watchmen guarding His TURAH and His NAME.

A choice between LIFE and DEATH

1 John 5:11–13

"And this is the witness: that Alahim has given us everlasting life, and this life is in His Son. He who possesses the Son possesses life, he who does not possess the Son of Alahim does not possess life. I have written this to you who believe in the Name of the Son of Alahim, so that you know that you possess everlasting life, and so that you believe in the Name of the Son of Alahim."

1 JOHN 5:11–1 BYNV

It is Yahusha that circumcises our hearts:

Kolossians 2:11–13

> *"in Him you were also circumcised with a circumcision*
> *NOT MADE WITH HANDS, in the putting off of the*
> *body of the sins of the flesh, by THE CIRCUMCISION*
> *OF MASHIAK, having been buried with Him in*
> *IMMERSION, in which you also were raised with*
> *Him through the belief in the working of Alahim, who*
> *raised Him from the dead. And you, being dead in your*
> *trespasses and the uncircumcision of your flesh, He has*
> *made alive together with Him, having forgiven you all*
> *trespasses."*
>
> KOLOSSIANS 2:11–13 BYNV

This act of immersion represents our circumcision, the outward sign or act of our belief, indicating the circumcision (cutting) of our hearts. Men boasting in one another's' flesh are missing the point. If we have received Yahusha's Ruach, we are His, and He has circumcised our hearts with a love for the Truth, a love for His Turah. If you have been circumcised with a circumcision not made with hands, you're done. Nothing you can do can improve on what Yahusha has done. This is how we can "obey from the heart."

Reprint with permission from BYNV www.TorahZone.net

What is the message?

The Besorah is the answer to mankind's oldest mystery, the purpose of life: to learn to love.

Active love is serving. From beginning to end, The Creator has pleaded, searched hearts, and repeated Himself beyond measure for mankind to return to Hm. Who has ears to hear Him? He said, "Love Me, and guard My Commandments." The Word, Light, Wisdom,

Living Water, and His Covenant are all one and the same thing: the Turah of Yahuah.

The Turah teaches us *how to love.*

Without love creation has no purpose. The Mashiak of Israel, Yahusha of Natsarith, told an elder of Yisharal:

"If you do not believe when I spoke to you about earthly things, how are you going to believe when I speak to you about the heavenly things? And no one has gone up into the heavens except He who came down from the heavens — the Son f Adam. And as Mosheh lifted up the serpent in the wilderness, even so much the Son of Adam be lifted up, so that whosoever believes in Him should not perish but possess everlasting life. For Alahim so loved the world that He gave His only procreated Son, so that everyone who believes in Him should not perish but possess everlasting life. For Alahim did not send His Son in to the world to judge the world, but that the world through Him might be saved. He who believes in Him is not judged, but he who does not believe is judged already, because he has not believed in the Name of the only procreated Son of Alahim.

And this is the judgment, that the light has come into the world, and men loved the darkness rather than the light, for their works were evil. For everyone who practices evil hates the light and does not come to the light, lest his works should be exposed. But the one doing the truth comes to the light, so that his works are clearly seen, that they have been wrought in Alahim." (Yahukanon 3)

"And He Himself is an atoning slaughter for our sins, and not for ours only but also for all the world. And by this we know that we know Him, if we guard His commands. The one who says, "I know Him," and does not guard His commands, is a liar, and the truth is not in him. But whoever guards His Word, truly the love of Alahim has been perfected in him. Bu this we know that we are in Him: The one who sys he stays in Him ought himself also t wolk, even as He walked. Beloved, I write no recent command to you, but an original command Two which you have had from the beginning, the original command is the Word which you head from the beginning." 1 Yakukanon.

(Turah is the original command)

Reprint with permission from BYNV page 17, www.TorahZone.net

Pledge of a good conscience toward Yahuah

1 Kefa 3:15–22

> *"But set apart Yahuah Alahim in your hearts, and always be ready to give an answer to everyone asking you a reason concerning the expectation that is in you, with meekness and fear, having a good conscience, so that when they speak against you as doers of evil, those who falsely accuse your good behavior in Messiah, shall be ashamed. For it is better, if it is the desire of Alahim, to suffer for doing good than for doing evil. Because even Messiah once suffered for sins, the obedient for the unobedient, to bring you to Alahim, having been put to death indeed in flesh but made alive in the Ruach, in which also He went and proclaimed to the ruachs in prison, who were disobedient at one time when the patience of Alahim waited in the days of Noah, while the ark was being prepared, in which a few, that is, eight beings, were saved through water, which figure (example) now also saves us: immersion — not a putting away of the filth of the flesh, but the pledge of a good conscience toward Alahim — through the resurrection of Yahusha Messiah, Who, having gone into heaven, is at the right*

hand of Yahuah, messengers and authorities and powers
having been subjected to Him."

1 KEFA 3:15–22

Shema

Deut 6:4–9

> *Hear, Yisharal: YAHUAH our Alahim, YAHUAH is one!*
> *And you shall love YAHUAH your Alahim with all your*
> *heart, and with all your being, and with all your might.*
> *And these Words which I am commanding you today*
> *shall be in your heart, and you shall impress them upon*
> *your children, and shall speak of them when you sit in*
> *your house and when you walk by the way, and when you*
> *lie down, and when you rise up, and shall bind them as a*
> *sign on your hand, and they shall be as frontlets between*
> *your eyes. And you shall write them on the doorposts of*
> *your house and on your gates.*
>
> DEUT 6:4–9 BYNV

Psalms 138:2

> *I bow myself toward Your qodesh Hekal and give thanks*
> *to Your Name for Your kindness and for Your truth; for*
> *You have made great Your Word, Your Name, above all.*
>
> PSALMS 138:2 BYNV

TaNaK

This acronym stands for Turah, Nabim, and Kethubim, or Instruction, Prophets, and Writings.

Turah, is often associated with the first FIVE BOOKS of Yahuah's Word. TURAH ... means INSTRUCTION TUROTH ... means INSTRUCTIONS Turah — Teaching, instruction BARASHITH

Books of the Beshorah of Yahusha

Genesis, (1 Mushah)

Shemoth (Exodus, 2 Mushah)

Uyiqara (FIRST WORD; "AND HE CALLED") (Leviticus, 3 Mushah)

Bamidbar (Numbers, 4 Mushah)

Debarim (Deuteronomy, 5 Mushah)

Yahusha (Joshua)

Shofetim (Judges, Rulers)

1 Shemual (1 Samuel)

2 Shemual (2 Samuel)

1 Malakim (1 Kings)

2 Malakim (2 Kings)

YashaYahu (Isaiah)

YirmeYahu (Jeremiah)

Yekezqal (Ezekiel)

Husha (Hosea)

Yual (Joel)

Amus AbadYah (Obadiah)

Yunah (Jonah)

Mikah (Micah)

Nakum (Nahum)

Kabaquq (Habakkuk)

Tsephanyah (Zephaniah)

Kagi (Haggai)

ZakarYah (Zekariah)

Tehillim (Psalms)

Mashal (Proverbs)

Ayub (Job)

Shir haShirim (Song of Songs)

Ruth Akah (Lamentations)

Qoheleth (Ecclesiastes,Convener)

Hadassah (Esther)

Ezra

NekemYah (Nehemiah)

1 Dibre haYamim (1 Kronicles, 1 Annals)

2 Dibre haYamim (2 Kronicles, 2 Annals)

Danial (Daniel)

Malaki (Malachi)

Natsarim writings (Also commonly called the BRITH KADASHA, Renewed Covenant Writings)

Yahukanon (John)

Yahudah (Jude)

Yaqub (James)

Luke Acts OF THE SPIRIT OF YAHUSHA

1 Kefa (1 Peter)

2 Kefa (2 Peter)

MatithYahu (Matthew) Mark

Romans

1 Korinthians

2 Korinthians

Galatians

Ephesians

Philippians

Kolossians

1 Thessalonians

2 Thessalonians

1 Timothy

2 Timothy

Titus

Philemon

Eberim (Hebrews)

1 Yahukanon (1John)

2 Yahukanon (2 John)

3 Yahukanon (3John)

Revelation

Reprint with Permission from BYNV

BYNU

𐤄𐤅𐤄𐤉 𐤏𐤔𐤅𐤄𐤉 RESTORED NAMES

BESORAH of YAHUSHA NATSARIM VERSION

LETTER STUDY CHART

LATIN		HEBREW	ARAMAIC			GREEK
A	**alef**	𐤀	א	1 ox	**alpha**	**A**
B	**beth**	𐤁	ב	2 house	**beta**	**B**
G	**gimel**	𐤂	ג	3 camel	**gamma**	Γ
D	**daleth**	𐤃	ד	4 door	**delta**	Δ
H	**hay**	𐤄	ה	5 window	**hoi**	H
U	**uau**	𐤅	ו	6 hook	**upsilon**	**Y**
Z	**zayin**	𐤆	ז	7 weapon	**zeta**	**Z**
CH	**heth**	𐤇	ח	8 fence	**(h)eta**	**H**
T	**teth**	𐤈	ט	9 winding	**theta**	Θ
Y	**yod**	𐤉	י	10 hand	**iota**	I
K	**kaph**	𐤊	כ	20 bent hand	**kappa**	K
L	**lamed**	𐤋	ל	30 goad	**lambda**	Λ
M	**mem**	𐤌	מ	40 water	**mu**	M
N	**nun**	𐤍	נ	50 fish	**nu**	N
S	**samek**	𐤎	ס	60 prop	**xei**	Ξ
E/A	**ayin**	𐤏	ע	70 eye	**omega**	Ω
P	**pe**	𐤐	פ	80 mouth	**pei**	Π
TS	**tsadee**	𐤑	צ	90 hook	**zeta**	**Z**
Q	**koph**	𐤒	ק	100 needle eye	**chi**	**X**
R	**resh**	𐤓	ר	200 head	**rho**	P
SH	**shin**	𐤔	ש	300 tooth	**sigma**	Σ
T	**tau**	𐤕	ת	400 mark	**tau**	T

BYNU - A HEBREW-ROOTS TRANSLATION

THE ORDER OF THE BOOKS IMPROVES UNDERSTANDING

TORAH INSTITUTE

TORAHZONE.NET

GLOSSARY

Adonai: Masoretes, used alternative vowels from another word, Adonai, in order to keep the Name of Yahuah concealed from the masses. The word Adonai was a "cue" to the reader not to Pronounce the Name!

Aleph/Tau: an Identity Mark, The WORD of Yahuah is one Person. He uses the first and last letters of the Hebrew alef-beth (alphabet) in specific location throughout the TaNaK to identify Himself as the One that is speaking.

Abrahim: Abram or AbuRamu (exalted father) renamed by Yahuah Abrahim, Father of Nations

Al, Alah: pronouns meaing the mighty, high, or lofty one.

Arets: earth, soil, land

Ash: male

Ashah: women

Baal, BEL: Lord, Aduni, owner; a word adopted as a proper noun (name) for the Kanaanite storm deity BEL (Baal), in Hebrew it is spelled BETH-AYIN-LAMED plural: Belim

Besorah: Message, testimony, report

Farah: [pe-resh-ayin-hay] usually seen as the Greek form, Pharaoh , a title for the ruler of Mitsrim (Egypt).

God: "Common Teutonic word for personal object of religious worship, formerly applicable to super-human being of heathen myth: on conversion of Teutonic race to Christianity, term was applied to Supreme Beings." *Encyclopedia Americans (1945 Edition)*

Hekal: Temple, Shrine The House built by Shalomoh, destroyed by Babylonians, rebuilt after return from Babel under governor, NekemYah

J E S U S: Jesus has not meaning in Hebrew and would have been unknown to Yahusha. Yahusha means Yah is our Deliverer or I am your Deliverer. The letter 'J' had not been invented during the time of Yahusha.

Lailah: Night, darkness

Lui: The name of the father of the tribe of priests

Lui; plural form Luim, commonly seen as LEVI, LEVITE; Aharon and Mosheh were Luim

Mashiak: The Christ, a title

Mosheh: Hebrew spelling: mem-shin-hay: draw-out

Mitsrites: Egyptians

Mitsrayim: Egypt

Mosheh: Moses

Nashim: Wives

Natsarim: Plural for Natsar. The original followers of Yahusha were the sect of the Natsarim (Acts 24:5). The word means watchmen, guardians, also used to mean branches. We are branches of the teachings of the Root.

Qodesh: Peculiar, special, precious, exceptional, distinctive, treasured above all, esteemed. (not KODESH, the word for month)

Renewed Covenant: is the Mashiak in you, the promised Paraklita (Helper) that comes into our hearts to inscribe His Turah on our hearts.

Ruach: Breath, wind, breeze, also known as spirit

Shabath [shin-beth-tau]: Rest, cease, complete shalom, the 7th day of each week, a sign forever between Yahuah and His people. It is the test given by Yahuah to determine who will obey Him, and is the sign of the eternal Covenant.

Shamayim: Skies, heavens. The word means lofty, and the second part of the word refers to "waters": the waters from which all creation began with.

Talmid: Student, pupil; plural form, talmidim

Turah: Instruction; plural form Turoth

Yahuah: 4 vowels: yod-hay-uau-hay. The Personal Name of our Creator, meaning: I will be there; I was, I am, I will be. Greek: Tetragrammaton (4 letters).

Yahusha: Name of Mashiak, means: Yah (I am) your Deliverer Yam,

Yamim: Lake, sea; yamim : seas

Yerushalayin: Jerusalem

YESHU: Yeshu is an acronym. (**Yemak Shmo U'Zikro**) The letters in this acronym mean: *may his name be blotted out.* A favored name of the enemy.

Yisharal: Y ("to") + SHAR ("rule") + AL (Alahim) means "to rule with Alahim." This elect group is often referred to in Scripture as the bride, or ashah, of Yahuah, the one body in Covenant with Him.

Yisharalites: Israelities

Yom, Yomim: Day, days; it is often and exact measurement of a night/day cycle, but the context may express figurative meaning, as "in those days," or when the Sun rises. Sunset is the end of each "day," and a new one begins in darkness, as it was in the beginning on the first day. "There was evening (darkness), and there was morning (boker), the first day."

Reprint from BYNV with permission.

ABOUT THE AUTHOR

Over the past 30 years Margaret St. Peter has been searching for truth and understanding. To know without a doubt eternal life was going to be a happy reality.

She was raised Catholic, then in her thirties started to explore Methodist, Assemblies of God, Baptist and non-denominational churches, never settling into any organized religion. Always feeling something was not quite right with what she was hearing from the pulpit. Luke 11:9 BYNV says: "Ask and it shall be given to you, seek and you shall find, knock and it shall be opened to you." That verse was a driving force for two decades as she focused on finding truth and understanding. Along the way she read hundreds of books, went to hear many teachers, and even earned a master's in theology.

Finally, Margaret found truth and understanding in the original Hebrew Scriptures. Secrets of the past were revealed. Secrets kept from the general population that contained amazing truth. Once truth is received one just has to share it.

Made in the USA
Las Vegas, NV
07 December 2022

61386734R00087